THE NAMES OF GOD

THE DAILY GRACE CO.

The Names of God
Copyright © 2022 by The Daily Grace Co.
Hanover, Maryland. All rights reserved.

Unless otherwise noted, all Scripture quotations are taken from the Christian Standard Bible®, Copyright © 2020 by Holman Bible Publishers. Used by permission. Christian Standard Bible® and CSB® are federally registered trademarks of Holman Bible Publishers.

The Daily Grace Co. exists to equip disciples to know and love God and His Word by creating beautiful, theologically rich, and accessible resources so that God may be glorified and the gospel made known.

Designed in the United States of America and printed in China.

*The more we know God,
the more we love Him.*

The Names of God

ABBA	08
ADONAI	12
ALMIGHTY	16
ALPHA AND OMEGA	20
ANCIENT OF DAYS	24
ANOINTED ONE	28
AUTHOR OF SALVATION	32
BREAD OF LIFE	36
BREATH OF LIFE	40
BRIDEGROOM	44
BRIGHT MORNING STAR	48
CHRIST, THE SON	52
CONSUMING FIRE	56
CORNERSTONE	60
DELIVERER	64
DWELLING PLACE	68
EL-DEAH	72
EL-KANNA	76
EL-ROI	80
ELOHIM	84
ETERNAL SPIRIT	88
EVERLASTING	92
FIRST AND LAST	96

FORTRESS	100
GOOD SHEPHERD	104
GREAT HIGH PRIEST	108
HIDING PLACE	112
HOLY ONE	116
I AM	120
IMMANUEL	124
JEHOVAH-JIREH	128
JEHOVAH-NISSI	132
JEHOVAH-RAPHA	136
JEHOVAH-SHALOM	140
KING	144
LAMB OF GOD	148
LIGHT OF THE WORLD	152
LIVING WATER	156
LORD OF ARMIES	160
MAN OF SORROWS	164
MIGHTY ONE	168
MOST HIGH	172
PRINCE OF PEACE	176
RABBI	180
SAVIOR	184
SHIELD	188
STRONG TOWER	192
THE VINE	196
WONDERFUL COUNSELOR	200
YAHWEH	204

INTRODUCTION

What is your name? This single question has laid the foundations for countless relationships to form. It is relevant no matter the place, culture, or time period in which it is asked. It is the question that allows communication to begin, conversation to flow, and connection to build. Once someone's name is known, every other fact learned about them is attached back to their name. *Brad is a proud grandfather. Deb is a compassionate mother. Susan is a hard worker.* Names define us and hold in themselves the defining qualities of who we are. And the names of God are no different.

Many people begin their relationship with God by asking, "God, who are you?" Thankfully, we can find the answer to that question in Scripture. God reveals His character, attributes, plans, purposes, and holiness to us through His Word—the Bible. He has most clearly revealed Himself through His Son, Jesus, who walked on the earth as fully man and fully God. But God also reveals Himself to us through other means. One of those means is the names He is called in Scripture. Scripture includes hundreds of names for God. This book contains in-depth descriptions of fifty of the most-used names of God in Scripture. Some names are ascribed to God the Father, some to Jesus the Son, and some to the Holy Spirit. Each one reveals a unique facet of who our triune God is and how He works.

There are many ways in which you can use this book. Perhaps it will serve as a helpful study resource during times of Bible reading and prayer, or maybe it will sit on your bedside table, readily available for the moments you need to be encouraged and reminded of the truth. However you decide to use this book, knowing, studying, and meditating on the names of God will help you grow, not only in your knowledge of God but in your personal relationship with Him. This is because the more we know God, the more we love Him. And what better way to get to know Him than by exploring His names—the very names revealed in Scripture.

May you know God more truly and love Him more deeply each time you open this resource to explore His names.

What comes into your mind when you think of the word "father"? What emotions do you feel? Maybe you feel a sense of warmth as you think of your father's arms hugging you tight. Maybe you feel the sting of sadness as you recall the sound of your father's car driving away, never to return. Maybe you feel a rush of anxiety as you remember the voice of the yelling father who hurt you. Or maybe you feel the ache of longing for the father you never knew.

The Bible calls God Abba, or Father. God is unlike the fathers of this world. Even the best father we could think of pales in comparison to the Father that God is.

The fathers of this world will fail us, but God never will.

He is not a father who hurts His children. He is not a father who abandons His children. He is not a father who is unable to be known by His children.

God is a Father who loves His children deeply and unconditionally.

While God loves all of His creation, only those who have a relationship with Him are considered His children. Romans 8:15–17 tells us that when we come to know Jesus, we are adopted as God's children. We become sons and daughters of the God of the universe. Now, whenever we think of God, our hearts cry out with joy, "Abba, Father!"

This relationship of sonship is a permanent relationship. When we come to faith in Jesus, we are adopted into God's family forever. Because the grace of Christ secures our position as God's children, we do not ever have to fear that we will lose God as our Father. We have received forgiveness and mercy through Christ, and this means we never have to be afraid that our Father will be mad at us when we mess up or that He will kick us out of His family for struggling with the same sin over and over again. Our position in God's family is a position that can never be taken away. He is ours, and we are His, forever.

As a good and loving Father, God has given gifts to His children. One of these gifts is simply a relationship with Him. We are known by God and have the opportunity to know God more and more as we study His Word. As we learn who God is through His Word, we see that He is a Father who is always with us — who cares for us when we feel broken and gives us His peace and strength. The character of God encourages us to run to Him when we are afraid, just like a little child runs to her father. Who God is reminds us that we can depend on Him and trust Him. All the best qualities found in earthly fathers are found in our heavenly Father — except, with our heavenly Father, these qualities are everlasting.

But one of the best gifts we have is a gift not fully received yet — an inheritance. In many families, especially in biblical times, fathers promise their children that they will one day receive the family's inheritance. In the same way, each of us who belongs to God receives an inheritance. This is not an inheritance of worldly gain but eternal gain—this inheritance is eternal life with our heavenly Father. While this inheritance is promised to us, we will not receive the fullness of this inheritance until Christ returns. One day, we will see our Father face-to-face and will dwell with Him for all of eternity.

Though our earthly relationship with our fathers may be painful, strained, or nonexistent, we have a relationship with our Abba, who cares for us, loves us, and remains with us. No matter how our earthly fathers make us feel,

we can remember and rest in the truth that we are wrapped in an eternal embrace with our heavenly Father.

Scripture for further study

MARK 14:36, ROMANS 8:15–17, GALATIANS 4:1–7

ADONAI

Each one of us experiences what it is like to submit to authority. Kids submit to the authority of their parents. Students submit to the authority of their teachers. Even full-grown, independent adults submit to the authority of their bosses or leaders. We submit to, or at least we are supposed to submit to, whoever has power over us.

But there is someone who has supreme authority, someone who is over even the highest of rulers and leaders—God. One of the names of God is Adonai, which translates as "Lord." It is interesting to note that, unlike the other names of God, Adonai is more of a title than a name. In the modern world, we can understand this as someone being called "President" or "Prime Minister." These designations are like a leader's name as they are how members of the public might address that person in power when referring to them. But still, the designations are not really a name—they are best understood as a title.

The title Adonai communicates God's sovereignty, the truth that He is Lord over all. However, God is not always viewed as the One who is Lord over all. Human authorities often see themselves as the ones in control. Even as individuals, we can often fight to be the ones in control. Our sinful nature causes us to naturally reject authority. Our flesh fights against submission and desires to be in charge. Although humans often view themselves as the ones who have power, the ones who rule and are in control, God is the One who reigns as Lord over everything.

It is when we are humbled by the circumstances of life that we realize we are in fact powerless. Our weaknesses, failures, and sins attest to the fact that we are helpless without the God who reigns. By His grace, God sent us Jesus so we could receive forgiveness and mercy for our rebellion and helplessness. As we submit to Christ and confess that He is Lord of our lives, we are given the Holy Spirit, who helps us fight the desire for control. The grace of Christ and the power of the Spirit help uncurl our fingers from our grip on control and bend our knees in submission to the Lord.

Each day for the believer requires submission to God. While our sinful flesh can make it difficult to submit to God daily, God's character encourages our submission to Him. We do not serve a God who is demanding, cruel, or unfair. The God we serve is compassionate, kind, and just. Unlike the rulers of this world, following and serving the Lord will never harm us or lead us astray. God rules with perfect justice and righteousness, which means His will and His commands are always good and right. Who God is leads us to trust Him. We can submit to the Lord with confidence, knowing that what God asks of us is for our good and His glory. Remembering the gospel also encourages our submission to God. It is not a duty but a delight to serve the God who loves us and gave Himself up for us.

When we recognize God as Lord, we discover comfort in unknown or troubling circumstances. Often, we fight for control because we want to feel like we are prepared for what we are experiencing or what is to come. We can sometimes fool ourselves into thinking that everything will turn out fine if we are the ones in control. But we fail to realize that we are imperfect and sinful. We do not have enough power in and of ourselves to hold everything together and ensure everything will go right—but God does. The supreme Lordship of God attests to His limitless power.

In times of uncertainty or trouble, we can relinquish our control to the God who has perfect control.

Instead of refusing to let go of the authority over our lives and plans, we can humbly yield to the God who knows and gives us what we need.

The holiness, righteousness, and grace of our God propels us to bow before Him as Lord.

One day, we will bow before the full presence of our Lord, but we can also bow to God right here and now as we submit to Him and trust His Lordship in our lives.

Scripture for further study

PSALM 8

ALMIGHTY

Have you ever felt the feeling of power? Have you ever felt like you could take on the world? Maybe you ran a marathon, and the endorphins rushing through your body gave you the feeling that you could conquer anything. Maybe you birthed a child, and after going through the pain of labor and delivery, you realized how much more powerful your body is than you previously thought. Or maybe you received a big promotion at work, which resulted in multiple subordinates coming under your authority and made you feel greater than the rest. Power is something that we, as humans, crave. We try to grasp it at every turn. Human ideas of power almost always exclusively deal with physical strength, physical resources, or demonstrations of explosive potential. God's power is often misunderstood because we tend to think of it in those ways.

However, God's power is much greater than our minds could even imagine.

In Scripture, God is called Almighty. This is how God revealed Himself to Abram in Genesis 17:1, saying, "I am God Almighty. Live in my presence and be blameless." The word "almighty" means "having complete power." Only God possesses transformative power, which is the power to sanctify His children and make us reflect the image of His Son. Only God possesses the power to protect and enable His people to do the impossible. And only God possesses resurrection power, which is the power that raised Jesus from the dead and raises our dead souls back to life. God changes people's lives dramatically and permanently. He

Let us accept our weakness so that we can lean into the One who is full of strength and power.

ordains events to accomplish what we could never do on our own. God uses His power on our behalf to accomplish His perfect will. And our faith is strengthened when we unmistakably see the work of God's power in our lives.

God's power is matchless because it is complete. The moments of power that we feel in our finite strength are nothing compared to the power of our God. As His children, we can rest in His power. We can continually be assured that His power is greater than our most intimidating trials. We can remember that He is the source of all power. What comfort is found in resting our lives in the hands of the Almighty God. And yet, what grace is lavished upon us when we desperately try to attain the power that only God possesses.

Let us accept our weakness so that we can lean into the One who is full of strength and power.

This is not a new idea, but it is a new way of living the life that God has always desired for His children — a life of dependence. In embracing our weakness, God's power is displayed.

Scripture for further study
GENESIS 35:11, JOB 5:17, PSALM 91:1

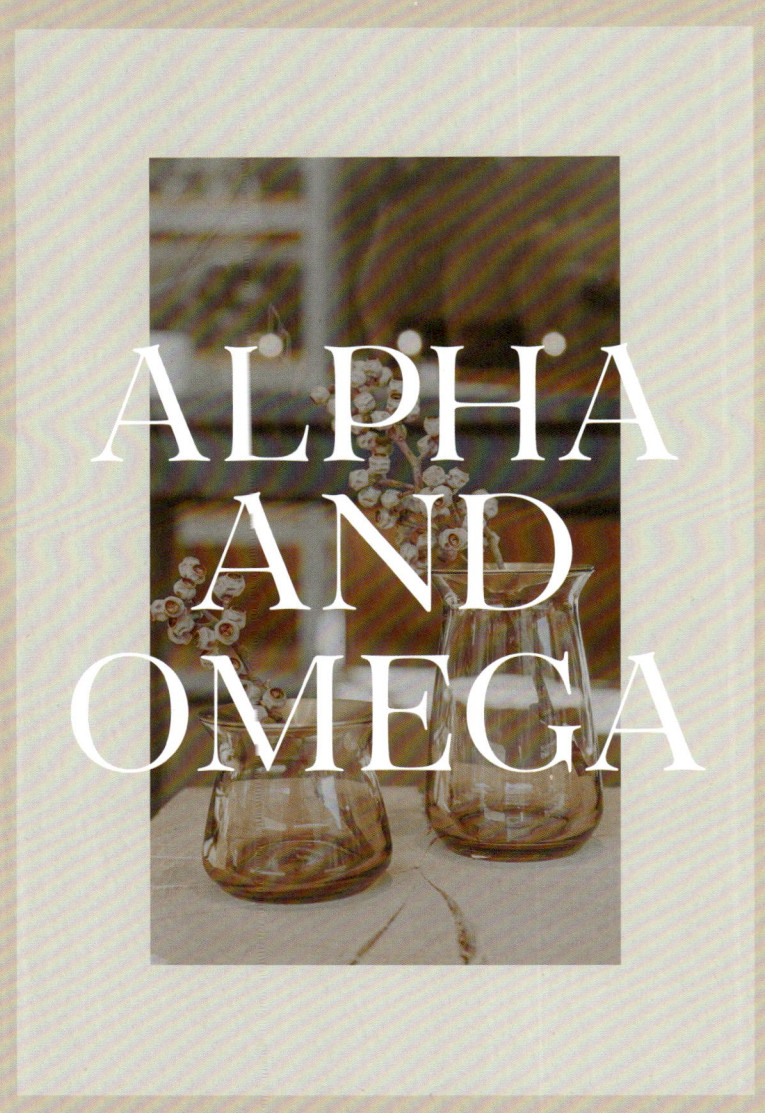

ALPHA AND OMEGA

There are two things that perplex the human mind: the beginning of life and the end of life. While daydreaming, we look up at the trees, the clouds, and the birds. We imagine the galaxies beyond earth and watch celestial bodies hover in thick darkness. We wonder what was before these creations. We try to trace back to the time before time, but our finite perspectives leave us with furrowed brows. Then, when reflecting on the end of days, we wonder how everything will come to its abrupt end. Will destructive earthquakes rise from the planet's core? Will fire fall from the skies? What will emerge from the debris and ruin? A new species for a new creation, perhaps? The human brain cannot know for sure on its own. It cannot see the final future, nor can it peer into the first past. It is bound to the present.

But God has been kind to our fallen minds and revealed to us the beginning and the end in Scripture. The Bible, which records God's words to His people, highlights that God Himself is the Alpha and Omega. The words *alpha* and *omega* are actually characters that signify the first and last letters in the Greek alphabet. Through the words of the Father and Jesus Christ, the triune God used these letters as His title in Scripture, declaring that He is the first and the last, the beginning and the end. From Genesis to Revelation, we do not just discover glimpses of pre-creation and the end times; we also gain an understanding of the One who has always been. We see a picture of God reigning eternally.

God existed before time, space, and matter. He is self-existent—He is who He is, independent from anything else. There was no other god before Him, and there was no time when He did not exist. For millennia upon millennia, God has been and

will be there. Everything came from His existence. He creates as the everlasting Creator. He sustains life as the never-failing Provider. And when the clock stops and the way of the world as we know it ceases, God will still exist. He will continue to be who He was at the beginning, for His character never changes.

Through the name Alpha and Omega, God shows His infinite nature to give us comfort.

When people change, cultures shift, and eras conclude, there is One on whom we can rely for eternity. He is our source of life forever. By Christ's saving work, we can always enjoy the blessing of God's presence. The truth of His presence is our firm foundation when we are confused by the past, and it is our hope when we are worried about the future. Because the eternal Son, Jesus Christ, will return to usher in the new heavens and earth, the end will be just the beginning for God's people. As a new creation, we who place our faith in Christ will meet our Savior and spend millennia upon millennia delighting in Him.

Scripture for further study

GENESIS 1:1–2, REVELATION 1,
REVELATION 21:1–8, REVELATION 22:12–13

ANCIENT OF DAYS

The name Ancient of Days has a nice ring to it and is often placed nicely in the lyrics of church hymns or written in beautiful liturgies. As a name of God, it is important to understand what it actually means. The name Ancient of Days is used a few times in the Bible, and each time, it is found in the book of Daniel. The first half of the book of Daniel focuses on Daniel's experience under the reign of four kings: King Nebuchadnezzar, King Belshazzar, King Darius, and King Cyrus. The second half of the book centers around Daniel's dreams and visions. The dreams and visions depict the end times during the establishment of God's full and final reign.

Daniel refers to the Ancient of Days multiple times in chapter 7 when explaining his dreams and visions, where he describes a courtroom scene in a time of future judgment. He sees a man who is God the Father seated on a flaming throne, with clothes as white as snow. His glory shines all around. He is seated with all authority over heaven and earth (Deuteronomy 4:39). And Daniel describes this scene in the best way words can depict, knowing it will never do justice to what he truly sees.

In his vision, the Son of Man approaches the Father on His throne. When Jesus Christ returns in His second coming, He will take the throne of God and reign supreme. The Father will give His Son keys to His eternal kingdom. The entire Bible points us to this moment, and Daniel reminds us that when this time comes, every person will be judged before the earth passes away and the new heavens and new earth are established. The living and the dead from all time will stand before the throne of God to receive His judgment.

The name Ancient of Days is a name used to describe God as the One who has seen it all.

God can perfectly judge because He has seen it all. He is eternal, the Ancient of Days. He is endless in nature and the treasure of all time. He is an eyewitness to every event in all of history. Because He is everywhere, knowing everything, from the beginning and end of time, God can administer true and just judgment like no one else. He can confirm or deny every charge. There is nothing that has escaped His knowledge or sight.

The name Ancient of Days is a name used to describe God as the One who has seen it all—from before the world began to every day right now and every day to come. God has been and will always be. He is the oldest of time, and yet He surpasses time. We can trust God in all He says and does because He has the fullest picture of our lives. He has the most all-inclusive knowledge of us, even before we entered the world. God's authority and eternal nature can bring us comfort today and every day because nothing under the sun is new to Him. His plan of redemption in Jesus Christ came with knowledge of everything that would transpire in this lifetime and after. We find hope in this truth, and we can entrust all of our days to the Ancient of Days.

Scripture for further study

DANIEL 7:9, DANIEL 7:13, DANIEL 7:21–22

ANOINTED ONE

In Bible times, it was a common practice to anoint oneself or others with oil. In the ancient near east, the sun was harsh, the climate hot, and the wind blew endlessly. People would rub oil on their faces, hands, and feet to protect and heal them from the elements (Matthew 6:17–18), and sometimes, a luxurious fragrance would even be added to the anointing oil. A host would honor and care for his guests by anointing their heads with oil when they arrived after their journey or, more rarely, anointing their feet, which undoubtedly took the biggest toll from the sand and heat.

Kings (1 Samuel 9:16), high priests (Leviticus 8:12), and prophets (Isaiah 61:1) were also anointed upon their commission or coronation. This practical ritual carried special meaning when it was used to identify people appointed by God to lead His people. To be anointed in this way meant to be set apart for a specific purpose by God. It was believed and often confirmed in Scripture that those God anointed to lead Israel carried an increased measure of the Spirit of God.

Throughout the Old Testament, and usually in response to moments of great sin, we see God promise to send a redeemer for Israel. This redeemer will be a specific person who is anointed and appointed to free God's people, both Jew and Gentile, from their bondage to sin and the punishment of death. Jesus is this Anointed One. He is not just someone who was anointed by God to lead His people for a time; Jesus is the Anointed One who has made a way for all God's people to have an intimate and personal relationship with God Himself.

Even the name Christ came from the Greek word for "anointed," which is *Christos*. Every time Jesus is called Christ in the Bible,

Jesus was anointed by God to redeem the world, and He accomplished that through His death and resurrection.

this is an affirmation that God chose and set apart Jesus to be the King of all kings and the Great High Priest. Likewise, the name Messiah originated from the Hebrew word *māšîah*, which was used to denote an anointed person. Scripture confirms that Jesus is the Anointed One by showing how He fulfills the Old Testament prophecies of the coming Messiah. For instance, He is the Son of David (Matthew 22:42), and He was born in Bethlehem (John 7:41–42), among many other prophetic fulfillments. We also know Jesus is the Anointed One because of His death on the cross and His resurrection back to life. Jesus's death was more than just physical death. The perfect blood He spilled paid for the sins of all mankind. And, though He laid breathless in a tomb for three days, He defeated sin and death forever when He arose to new life. Jesus was anointed by God to redeem the world, and He accomplished that through His death and resurrection.

Jesus is also the One anointed to transform the kingdom of this world into the kingdom of the Lord (Revelation 11:15). Jesus is appointed to judge between those who belong to Him and those who belong to the accuser (Revelation 20:4). He will return to the earth one day to vanquish all sin, defeat all evil, and make heaven and earth new (Revelation 21:1). Jesus is the Anointed One of God. It is through Him that God is redeeming and will restore all things!

Scripture for further study

PSALM 2:2, DANIEL 9:25, JOHN 1:41, JOHN 4:25,
ACTS 4:27, ACTS 10:38, HEBREWS 1:9, REVELATION 11:15

AUTHOR OF SALVATION

God created the stars, the moon, and the sun. He made rolling hills, endless plains, and high mountains. He made birds that fly, fish that swim, and human beings that reflect His image. The creation account says He rested after forming the earth and all things on it. But He was not done creating new things just yet.

He also created salvation. Why? Because He created all of His creation to bring glory to His name for the purpose of serving Him. Yet, when Adam and Eve sinned, they did the opposite of what they were created to do. They exalted the deceiver, Satan, and served themselves by choosing what they wanted over what God commanded. Their choice led to death for them and all human beings after them. Yet God had a plan to offer life to those sentenced to death for their sin. He authored salvation.

The name Author of Salvation is used in Scripture to describe God. The Greek word for "author" is *archēgos*. *Archēgos* can mean many things, but all meanings have the same intended connotation. The first half of the word, *archē*, is a prefix that means to "begin or initiate action." The second half of the word, *gos*, further defines the word to not just refer to initiating action but also continuing to lead it. Therefore, *archēgos* has been translated to mean "author, captain, founder, pioneer, originator, or leader." An author both dreams up the idea for a book but also writes and edits the words in it until they perfectly communicate the intended idea. The captain of a boat launches a vessel into the water, but he also charts the course of the journey ahead, makes critical decisions when issues arise, and commands the entire crew on how to work together to sail safely to the destination. As such, *archēgos* implies a type of leadership that pioneers a new way forward and leads others to follow that way. Jesus pioneered

God had a plan to offer
life to those sentenced
to death for their sin.
He authored salvation.

a new way to the Father when He gave His life on the cross to pay the debt of sin for all who believe in Him. In doing this, He authored new life! He is even called the Author of Life because it is from Him that all life, both physical and spiritual, flows (Acts 3:15 ESV).

Not only is God the originator and Jesus the founder of salvation, but the Holy Spirit leads and guides us to salvation in Christ and shows us how to live worthy of the resurrection from the dead we have received. God created salvation. He initiated it because He loves people and does not want them to perish but to be cleansed of their sin and united with Him in eternity. Salvation is a gracious provision God chose to provide to all who will believe. Jesus was the first to show us what salvation looked like. He died on a cross, yet He did not stay dead. He rose again to life and defeated sin forever. Jesus first lived a resurrected life.

Salvation is not something that can be started or secured by human effort. It begins and endures only by the will of God. Salvation depends only on the love, faithfulness, and righteousness of God. Therefore, even when we are weak and weary, we cannot be separated from salvation if we have repented of our sin and believed in Jesus, the Author of Salvation.

Scripture for further study

ACTS 3:15, ACTS 5:31, HEBREWS 2:10, HEBREWS 12:2

BREAD OF LIFE

Imagine coming to a dining table after days without food. Perhaps you are a weary traveler who has suffered famine. Or maybe you are mourning a loss and have not been able to bring yourself to eat. You pull your chair across a woven rug and feebly sit. The table has an abundance of food before you. At the center is a large loaf of bread split in half. Steam rises from its air pockets, and the flaky crust shines its golden brown color. The dinner host gives you a slice. As you chew and swallow, that piece of bread immediately gives your malnourished body sustenance. It fills you with warmth and satisfaction.

Jesus calls Himself the Bread of Life. In John 6:35, He said, "I am the bread of life. . . . No one who comes to me will ever be hungry, and no one who believes in me will ever be thirsty again." This statement was challenging for many listeners at the time, as Jesus continued to teach that the one who feeds on His flesh would live (John 6:53–58). Through His language, Jesus exposed hardened hearts but pointed to Himself as the solution for those in need. However, Jesus was not addressing a physical need or a physical hunger. Rather, Jesus is bread to fill a spiritual need, a spiritual hunger for righteousness. He offered His sacrificed body like a broken loaf on a dining table. It is the only thing to save a malnourished soul.

Have you hungered for righteousness? Are you tired from wandering away from God, seeking dessert in a world full of rocks? Have you suffered from loss or experienced so much sorrow that you have forgotten the taste of goodness? There is bread to eat; it is the staple and essential part of your diet. For those from different cultural backgrounds, you may consider rice, lentils, or potatoes. In every type of sustenance, Jesus meets with all of

Jesus invites us to His table. Will you come?

us who place our faith in Him. Jesus invites us to His table. Will you come? There, you will not be expected to leave when the meal concludes. You have a seat sealed in eternity.

Christ, the Bread of Life, will always be there to give us relief from sin and brokenness.

However, it is important to note that the Bread of Life must be consumed to receive the nutrients necessary for growth and well-being. We must "consume" Christ to benefit from His saving work, to have a new life and a Christlike nature. In other words, we must be united to Jesus in a way that mirrors the union between food and our bodies. The Spirit of Jesus gives nutrients to our souls just as food gives nutrients to our body's cells. We need this grace daily as we continue to navigate a famished land. We can eat again and again when we turn to the Scriptures and reflect on the gospel. And we can point other wanderers and sufferers to Christ's table while making the Bread, which allows us to be finally full, known to the world.

Scripture for further study
JOHN 6:22–59

BREATH OF LIFE

Then he said to me, "Son of man, can these bones live?" I replied, "Lord God, only you know." He said to me, "Prophesy concerning these bones and say to them: Dry bones, hear the word of the Lord. This is what the Lord God says to these bones: I will cause breath to enter you, and you will live." (Ezekiel 37:3–5)

To breathe is to be alive. These two things go hand in hand as one ceases to exist without the other. Breathing is not something we have to remember to do. We inhale and exhale on cue without having to rehearse the mechanics of the action itself. And yet, this simple thing we do all day, every day, is evidence of our very existence.

Our God is called the Breath of Life because He is the source and sustainer of all creation. He holds all things, including our existence, in His loving and sovereign hands. God accomplishes the impossible by giving life to that which was previously dead. He called the prophet Ezekiel to proclaim His Word, not to people but to a valley full of dry, lifeless bones. As Ezekiel preached God's Word, God laid flesh and skin over the bones. These newly created bodies, though divinely fashioned, were still as lifeless as before until God breathed His life into them (Ezekiel 37:10). Ezekiel experienced the impossible. He witnessed the Breath of Life at work.

This vision is a beautiful expression of God's redemptive love. In a great reversal, God brought life out of death. The bones could not muster up the strength to be alive again. They were as dead as they could be. In the same way, we cannot sustain ourselves, physically or spiritually, in our own strength. We are unable to add days to our lives. No amount of good works

Each inhale and exhale is an exercise in God's sustaining power over your life.

can make us right before a holy God. The Breath of Life does what we cannot do for ourselves. He replaces our heart of stone with a heart of flesh (Ezekiel 36:26), making us spiritually alive, no longer bound by the effects of death in our lives. This great reversal from death to life brings comfort to us now in difficult circumstances and provides unwavering hope for the life to come.

The Breath of Life does the impossible by redeeming all that is beyond repair and without hope. Adam experienced the impossible back in the garden of Eden when God created his body out of dust and breathed life into him. Mary Magdalene witnessed the impossible when Jesus stood in front of her only days after He breathed His last breath on the cross. We see God do the impossible today as the Holy Spirit enters the lives of people dead in their sin and makes them spiritually alive. And we look forward to the day when God will do the impossible again when He returns to resurrect the dead and usher in the new heavens and the new earth.

From creation to new creation, the Breath of Life is continually at work. Each inhale and exhale is an exercise in God's sustaining power over your life. Your salvation is a gift. Your eternal security is a miracle. Rejoice in God, the Breath of Life, for His work in making all things new, including you. He restores all that is broken. The old has passed away, and behold, the new has come (2 Corinthians 5:17).

Scripture for further study

GENESIS 2:7, JOB 33:4, EZEKIEL 37:1–28

BRIDEGROOM

A wedding is a beautiful occasion to celebrate the union between a man and a woman. Romance is in the air as the music slowly plays and the lights dim. Elegant tablecloths and drapes hang gracefully. Flower arrangements transform the space into a garden paradise. Attendees wait with expectation to see the bride adorned in white and jewelry. But they are not the ones with the most anticipation. The groom, also sometimes called the bridegroom, is the one most excited to see his bride. He stands at the altar, nervous. His palms sweat, and his heart races. The voices around him become background chatter, and all other faces blur together. The only thing on his mind is the radiance of his love. He focuses on her arrival at the other end of the aisle. He remembers the proposal and the covenant relationship he initiated. Regardless of whatever challenges come, the bridegroom is ready to vow his life to his bride's well-being and protection.

God calls Himself the Bridegroom to His people. Through the Holy Spirit's inspiration, various biblical authors used Bridegroom as a name of God to illustrate His commitment, pursuit, sacrificial love, and fierce loyalty to His people. Isaiah 62:5 states, "For as a young man marries a young woman, so your sons will marry you; and as a groom rejoices over his bride, so your God will rejoice over you." God initiated a covenant, which is a binding promise, with His people. It was first relayed to the Israelite patriarch, Abraham. In the covenant, God declared that He would bless Abraham's descendants by giving them a place in His presence and making them a great nation (Genesis 12:1–3, 15, 17). Like the vows of a marriage ceremony, God vowed to forever be their God, and they would be His people.

*His passion never
fades, and His covenant
commitment never fails.*

But the people of God were like a runaway bride. Throughout redemptive history, we see how they rejected their gracious Lord. The Israelites fell from their commitment and fell into sin. Adulterous, they chased after other gods. Their pattern of disloyalty continues in our hearts. God predestined us to receive His love, and through our faith, we become Abraham's descendants, the Lord's Bride. However, we too reject the covenant blessings and our relationship with our Covenant-Maker when we sin. Despite our rebellion, the Bridegroom remains faithful to His word, as recorded in Scripture. As the Old Testament prophets predicted, God promised to remove the desire for disobedience from our hearts and enable us to love Him only. God fulfilled this promise through the Bridegroom, who left His throne to pursue us.

Jesus Christ was this Bridegroom. He pursued us to the point of death by crucifixion. He did this so that our covenant violations would be forgiven and so that we would be reconciled to God. In Christ's sacrifice, we see God's immense love for us. We can trust that nothing will ever separate us from this love. It is the most powerful thing. Because Christ is our Bridegroom, we know we are secure in God. Our Bridegroom chose us and always delights in us. His passion never fades, and His covenant commitment never fails.

Scripture for further study

ISAIAH 62:5, HOSEA 2:16–20, MATTHEW 9:14–15, EPHESIANS 5:25–27, REVELATION 19:6–8

BRIGHT MORNING STAR

Astronomers call the planet Venus "the morning star." Among all the celestial bodies in the night's sky, Venus shines the brightest. Even in thick darkness, an observer can pick out the radiant planet. He or she does not need any telescope. Venus will be easy to identify right after sunset and right before sunrise and will always be there, guiding the stargazer. However, Venus's light is not its own. As a planet, Venus does not produce or emit its own light as an actual star does. Rather, planets reflect the light of the star around which they rotate. Because it rotates the sun, Venus actually reflects sunlight. Though captivating, its bright appearance is only a shadow of something greater.

The science behind this name also has biblical significance. The prophet Isaiah called the nation Babylon the "shining morning star" (Isaiah 14:12). In Scripture, a star represents divinity. Though it was an earthly kingdom, Babylon sought a divine destiny through its many military conquests. The kings of Babylon used warfare to capture other nations in pursuit of eternal authority. Babylon was a wicked kingdom and later became a symbol of spiritual evil. Under King Nebuchadnezzar, Babylon destroyed the kingdom of Judah, which was God's holy nation. But God promised to restore His nation again, and He would punish Babylon for its destruction.

Through Isaiah, the Lord predicted that Babylon would "fall from heaven." Its mission to obtain a divine and eternal destiny would be halted. Though it appeared like a star, Babylon was just a planet; it dimly reflected the light of the greatest kingdom, the kingdom of God. Though it seemed the brightest of all the nations, Babylon was like Venus, which is only the brightest for a short period before the sun overshadows it. In

As the true Morning Star, Jesus cannot be defeated or overshadowed.

time, Babylon and all spiritual evil would be overshadowed by the true star of heaven: the Son of God.

Jesus calls Himself the Bright Morning Star in Revelation 22:16. Old Testament prophecy predicted that a star would come out of Israel and reign in righteousness (Numbers 24:17). He would crush the head of evil and establish God's good kingdom on earth. By His saving work, Jesus proved to be this promised star. The Father gave Jesus all divine and eternal authority. As the true Morning Star, Jesus cannot be defeated or overshadowed. His light is from His own nature. From His throne, He continues to rule in power.

When we look at the stars, we should be drawn to the One they reflect. For now, the celestial bodies are amazing to gaze upon and are necessary for light. But there will be a time when the sun, the moon, and the planets will no longer be the most awe-inspiring objects in the sky. There will be a time when their radiance will no longer be needed (Revelation 21:23). When Christ returns, His brightness will forever captivate our attention. His light will be stronger than all the objects in the sky, for His fully-revealed glory will guide us to Himself.

Scripture for further study

NUMBERS 24:17, MATTHEW 2:2, REVELATION 2:26–28, REVELATION 21:23, REVELATION 22:16

CHRIST, THE SON

One of the most seemingly audacious claims Jesus made during His ministry was that He was the Son of God. Jesus often referred to God as His Father, which caused quite a stir among the people, especially the religious leaders. What made this claim so audacious in the eyes of the religious leaders was that calling God one's Father implied a relationship of equality. John records in John 5:18, "This is why the Jews began trying all the more to kill him: Not only was he breaking the Sabbath, but he was even calling God his own Father, making himself equal to God." While a father-son relationship between humans implies likeness but not equality, Jesus's declaration—that He is the Son and God is His Father—implies both likeness and equality. Because Jesus is the Son of God, He is God.

The truth that Christ is the Son holds significant implications. First, Jesus being the Son confirms that Jesus is God. Many people today seek to discredit the deity of Jesus, but God's Word declares the truth of Christ's deity. Jesus is God, the second member of the Trinity, who shares perfect equality with God. Christ's Sonship also speaks to the love God and Jesus share with one another. A perfect father-son relationship is a relationship of intimacy, and this is the relationship Jesus and God share. We see evidence of this love between God and Jesus when Jesus is baptized, and God boasts from heaven: "You are my beloved Son; with you I am well-pleased" (Mark 1:11).

While the love Jesus and God share is unique, Christ made it possible for us to experience a similar type of relationship with God. John 3:16 tells us how we can see God's expression of His love for the world through His giving up of His Son to die for us. Unlike some sons who are disobedient to their fathers, Jesus

We are able to have a relationship with our heavenly Father and experience the great love He has for us.

was the perfectly obedient Son. He took on the punishment we deserved for our sin by dying on the cross. He experienced the pain of His Father turning away from Him because of the sin that was upon Him. Because of Christ's death and resurrection, those who repent and trust in Him are forgiven of their sin. But one of the most special gifts Christ bestows on those who come to know Him is the gift of sonship. Romans 8:14 says, "For all those led by God's Spirit are God's sons." The Son of God enables us to be sons of God.

For those of us in Christ, we share a relationship of intimacy with our Father. The tender relationship between a father and son is something we get to experience as God's children. Just as the Father and the Son know one another deeply, we are known by our God and able to know Him in return. Because of Christ, we also have fellowship with the Son. The relationship we have with Jesus means that we daily walk with the Son and experience His strength, peace, and help. All of these blessings are possible because of the person and work of Jesus Christ. By God's grace, we are able to know the Son, walk with the Son, and one day live with the Son for eternity. Because of Christ the Son, we are able to have a relationship with our heavenly Father and experience the great love He has for us.

Scripture for further study

MATTHEW 27:54, JOHN 1:11–12, JOHN 15:1–10

CONSUMING FIRE

Fire can be a polarizing force. On the one hand, fire can provide warmth, purification, and the ability to cook our food. On the other hand, when left unattended, fire can devour and destroy everything in its path. Humans need fire, but we also fear it. The same can be said of God—we need Him, but we also fear Him. This is not a fear that sends us cowering in a corner; it is a reverent fear that has us on our knees, worshiping our holy God who holds the world in His hands. Scripture tells us that "our God is a consuming fire" (Hebrews 12:29). His fire is glorious, just, holy, loving, and also wrathful.

God is called a Consuming Fire ten times throughout Scripture. The three main aspects of His character on display in these references are His glory, His wrath, and the reverent fear He is due. The first place we read about God as a Consuming Fire is in Exodus 24. The Israelites had left their bondage in Egypt, and Moses was leading them toward the Promised Land when they stopped at the foot of Mount Sinai. It was there that God renewed His covenant with Moses and the nation of Israel. This covenant expanded on the very promises made to Abraham and continued the covenant of grace that would find fulfillment in Jesus. At the foot of Mount Sinai, God commanded Moses to go up the mountain to receive the Law. As Moses climbed the mountain, "The appearance of the Lord's glory to the Israelites was like a consuming fire on the mountaintop" (Exodus 24:17). Moses was enveloped by the glory of the Lord and stayed on the mountain for forty days and nights. God's glorious presence consumed Moses as he received the Law from the Lord. Moses experienced

God's glory personally, while the Israelites could see it from the foot of the mountain. Even then, it was just a small taste of His glory that fills the universe even now.

The words "consuming fire" are also used to describe the devouring wrath of God. To understand this aspect of God's character, we have to remember He is holy and cannot be in the presence of sin. He must punish sin; therefore, His wrath is complete and devastating. Isaiah 29:6 describes this, as it says, "you will be punished by the Lord of Armies with thunder, earthquake, and loud noise, storm, tempest, and a flame of consuming fire." For those who are not covered in the sacrificial blood of Christ, this consuming fire of wrath is a future reality. One day, when Christ returns and takes His children home, the earth as we know it will be consumed in fire.

God will purify His creation that has been marred by sin. His consuming fire will make all things new.

Lastly, knowing God as our Consuming Fire brings us to our knees in reverence and awe of who He is. We are called to fear Him because He "is a consuming fire, a jealous God" (Deuteronomy 4:24). In Deuteronomy 4, Moses speaks to the Israelites before they enter the Promised Land. In his message, he warns them to keep idols from their lives. God has made and kept His covenant to the nations. In return, He expects true worship and devotion. He will not share His glory with other gods. True fear of the Lord is not cowering in terror over what God can do to you in His wrath; it is worshiping Him because of what He has done for you through Christ. We are reminded of this in Proverbs 14:26–27, which says, "In the fear of the Lord one has strong confidence and his children have a refuge. The fear of the Lord is a fountain of life, turning people away from the snares of death." To fear our Consuming Fire is to bring life and refuge. In His great mercy, God sent Jesus to take the wrath we deserve.

Because of our Savior's sacrifice, we now joyfully welcome the Consuming Fire to envelope our hearts and lives.

Scripture for further study
EXODUS 24, DEUTERONOMY 4:15–31, HEBREWS 12:18–29

CORNERSTONE

If you have ever played a game of Jenga, you know how essential it is to have a steady block that keeps the tower together. Even if other blocks are removed, the strong block keeps the tower from crumbling. But, once that one important block is taken out, the whole tower comes crashing down. Jesus is like the essential block, for He is our Cornerstone. A cornerstone is a stone at a corner of a building's foundation that holds that building together. This cornerstone is necessary to keep the structure steady, and without it, the building would not hold together well at all. Jesus is our Cornerstone because He is not only the foundation of our faith, but He is the One who keeps our faith firm. Without Jesus's death and resurrection, there would be no basis for our faith. There would be nothing upon which our faith could hinge. Just like that critical piece in a Jenga tower, without Jesus, we would crumble.

As a cornerstone shapes a building, so Jesus shapes believers into a building for the Lord. Ephesians 2:19–22 paints a wonderful picture of this truth. Paul describes how, as believers, we belong to the family of God. As His family, we are put together to form a building, "a holy temple in the Lord," with Jesus as our Cornerstone. Peter also speaks to this truth in 1 Peter 2:4–5. He tells us, "As you come to him, a living stone—rejected by people but chosen and honored by God—you yourselves, as living stones, a spiritual house, are being built to be a holy priesthood to offer spiritual sacrifices acceptable to God through Jesus Christ." Believers are like living stones, being formed together to be a holy house for God. But we would not be this holy temple without the foundation and formation of Christ. He is the One who caused us to become living stones in the first place, and He is the One who builds us up by the Spirit.

As our Cornerstone, Jesus keeps us permanently steady and secure.

Yet, even though we have been shaped by Christ, others stumble over Christ. Peter continues in 1 Peter 2:6–8 by describing how people rejected Jesus and stumbled over His teachings rather than accepting them. Even today, we see how many people reject the gospel and allow their sin and pride to cause them to stumble over the truth. But Jesus is not defeated or disarmed by the rejection of man. Even though Jesus was rejected by those He came to save, God was still faithful to use Him to bring salvation. By His work on the cross, Jesus became our Cornerstone. While it is discouraging to know that others stumble over the truth rather than receive it, we can be grateful for the salvation we have received by relying on our Cornerstone.

Because Jesus holds us together, we can lean on Him to keep us steady. We can ask Him to continue to build us up in our faith, to shape us into vessels of worship for the Lord. We can pray for Him to make Himself known to those who reject Him so that they, too, would come to know Christ as their Cornerstone. And, when we feel shaken and like everything around us is falling apart, we can cling to Him, our solid foundation. With Jesus, we will never be torn down, no matter what seeks to destabilize us. As our Cornerstone, Jesus keeps us permanently steady and secure.

Scripture for further study

PSALM 118:22, ISAIAH 28:16, ACTS 4:10–12

DELIVERER

God has been a Deliverer from the very beginning. From the first pages of the Bible, we see God take a dark and chaotic world and form it into a place of light and life. As the story of Scripture unfolds, we see God continue to be a Deliverer as He rescues Noah from the waters of the flood, Lot from the destruction of Sodom and Gomorrah, the Israelites from the hardship of slavery, and the list goes on. Though humanity is sinful and rebellious against God,

by His grace and mercy, God continues to deliver. He is a God who rescues and redeems.

God's deliverance is connected with salvation. Each instance of God's deliverance in the Bible describes God's mighty hand to bring His people out of a situation of wickedness, trouble, or hopelessness. God's deliverance in Scripture proclaims the power of God to save, no matter the circumstance. Although God's people often place themselves in situations from which they need rescue, God rescues them every time.

Each instance of deliverance in the Old Testament whispers of the deliverance God would one day bring through Jesus Christ. Jesus is our Great Deliverer. Each one of us needs rescue because of the punishment we are due for our sin and rebellion against God. We are unable to deliver ourselves on our own, but by His grace and mercy, Jesus reaches down into our place of despair and delivers us. Therefore, the salvation we have received through Christ is an act of deliverance. The grace and mercy of God, given to us

God's deliverance in Scripture proclaims the power of God to save, no matter the circumstance.

through the death and resurrection of Christ, has delivered us from the domain of darkness and transferred us to the kingdom of God (Colossians 1:13 ESV).

However, even those of us who have received salvation through Christ still yearn for deliverance today. We live in a world that is dark and broken, and we crave to be rescued from this place. Yet there is hope. Just as God did not leave His people in a place of wickedness or despair, God will not leave us in this world of brokenness. One day, Christ will return to deliver us completely. He will restore creation to a place of complete peace and harmony. No longer will we live in a world tainted by sin, for God's restoration will make all things new.

This is the hope that we cling to when we feel the longing for deliverance. No matter what ails us today—whether it be anxiety, a bodily disorder, or a situation of injustice—there is peace to be found as we rest in the deliverance that is to come. While God can bring deliverance on this side of eternity, we can hold on to hope, even if our situation persists, because of the promised deliverance on the other side. God will bring us out of every ache and every trial. Though the waiting can feel long and the pain can feel strong, our God is coming to rescue us. God has been a Deliverer from the very beginning, and He will deliver us in the very end.

Scripture for further study
2 SAMUEL 22:2–3, PSALM 34:17

DWELLING PLACE

God desires to dwell with us in love and fellowship. Though sin has separated us from His physical presence on earth, God's people still enjoy His spiritual presence through salvation in Jesus Christ, our Lord and Savior.

> *Jesus provides safety, comfort, and fullness of joy in this life when we find our dwelling in Him.*

And, when He comes again at the end of time, we will dwell with God in a physical and spiritual sense forever.

Psalm 91:1 says, "The one who lives under the protection of the Most High dwells in the shadow of the Almighty." The name Dwelling Place is used for God throughout the Bible. The word translated "dwelling place" in the original Hebrew language means "refuge, habitation, shelter." And the words "to dwell" in the Hebrew language mean to "remain in." This definition does not mean visiting occasionally; it encourages us to abide, to live, and to make our home in God's presence. For the Christian, enjoying and dwelling in the presence of God is the greatest necessity. It is the means by which we commune and fellowship with God.

We often are inclined to make a dwelling place in other things that cannot uphold the weight of our need—relationships, success, wealth, possessions, and other false comforts. We may look to these things when we need help or desire to seek refuge from the hardships of life. But, when we seek shelter in any other place, person, or thing apart from God, we will find insufficient comfort and refuge when we need it most.

Dwelling in God's presence shapes everything about our lives

—the way we work, the way we conduct our relationships, the way we speak, the way we think, the way we serve, and everything we do. We dwell in Him by relying and depending on Him with all things, by spending time with Him, by reading about Him in His Word, and by centering our lives around Him. God gives us access to His divine power and provides us with everything we need for life and godliness (2 Peter 1:3). Why would we search for help and refuge anywhere else? When we remain in the Lord, nothing in this life can shake us and defeat us. God is all-sufficient. He keeps us safe in His comfort and care, and He helps us endure through all of life's circumstances and challenges.

The importance of dwelling with the Lord is illustrated in Psalm 27:4–5, which says, "I have asked one thing from the Lord; it is what I desire: to dwell in the house of the Lord all the days of my life, gazing on the beauty of the Lord and seeking him in his temple. For he will conceal me in his shelter in the day of adversity; he will hide me under the cover of his tent; he will set me high on a rock." In these verses, the psalmist expresses his one true desire: to dwell with God. He believes in the sufficient power and perfect provision of the Lord. He runs to God without delay and finds his greatest confidence and delight with the Lord. How many of us can say the same?

God provides us the opportunity every moment of every day to find comfort in His presence, to dwell safely in His midst, and to enjoy His presence. Even as the world bombards us with troubles and circumstances that try to disrupt our peace,

God covers us with His presence. He is our shelter, refuge, and strength. He is our dwelling place.

Scripture for further study
DEUTERONOMY 33:27, PSALM 84:1–4, PSALM 91:9–10

EL-DEAH

"Why?" We often start asking this question as curious children and continue asking it as bewildered adults. Many of us are familiar with the adage that says, "with age comes wisdom," yet it may be more true to say that with age comes an understanding of how much wisdom we lack. We cannot explain much of our life circumstances. Why this sickness? Why this pain? Why this heartbreak? Why must we wait? We want wisdom, knowledge, and understanding on these issues. We think if we can just understand, then maybe we can cope with and even embrace the hardships handed to us. But, if we want knowledge, then perhaps instead of seeking answers, we should be seeking God.

God is knowledge. He is El-Deah, translated from Hebrew as "the God of knowledge." He is the only One who knows all things. Truly, *all things*. The earth itself was founded by His knowledge (Proverbs 3:19–20). Think about that for a moment. Everything you see, touch, taste, hear, and smell was created by the knowledge of God. No nanoparticle or galaxy took shape without Him speaking it into being from the wisdom within Him.

The thought of God knowing all things and creating all things from His knowledge is mind-blowing. And rightly so, because the Bible tells us

the knowledge of God is beyond what we are capable of understanding.

Romans 11:33 reflects on the depths of the riches and the wisdom and the knowledge of God, making clear that His judgments are unsearchable. The depths of God's wisdom are like the deepest parts of the ocean, where no light breaks in and no man could possibly reach. And because God's wisdom is so deep, it also means His ways are impossible to understand. When we come to a situation in which we cannot comprehend why God is moving and working in the way He is, we should not be surprised.

Our God wills and works according to His infinite knowledge.

We cannot and will not ever understand His wisdom or His ways in full. He is El-Deah. We are merely the work of the hands of El-Deah.

Fascinatingly, the knowledge of God is discussed endlessly in the book of Job by Job and his friends Eliphaz, Bildad, and Zophar. Aside from Jesus, Job arguably experienced more suffering, loss, and pain than anyone in the Bible. And Job and his friends debated the reason for this suffering at great length. Had Job earned his suffering by sinning against God? Was God angry with Job? Was God recklessly throwing hardship Job's way?

After many chapters of debate over the question of "Why?", God finally intervenes and speaks to Job. Only God never tells Job the reason he lost his children, home, health, and livelihood. Instead, God reminds Job of His surpassing power and greatness. It was God who established the earth, fixed its dimensions, supports its foundations, and laid its cornerstone (Job 38:4–6). God was just as in control of Job's life as He was in the creation of the world. God was asking Job to trust Him even when Job could not understand. Understanding our circumstances only gives us temporary peace. There will always be new circumstances that arise and demand a new explanation. However, the knowledge of God never fades. We will never know all the answers, but He does. We must trust in Him, El-Deah, and not in the answers we may or may not ever receive.

God is the God of knowledge, and for that reason, we can fully trust Him. He knows and understands what we do not. He knows all things that have been, are, and will be. And He has hidden all the mysteries of the knowledge of Him in Christ. When we enter into a relationship with God by grace through faith in Jesus, we are invited into the treasure of wisdom and knowledge in Him (Colossians 2:2–3). We will never fully understand God, but all who believe are invited into the riches of personally knowing El-Deah through Christ. What a precious gift that is for those in Christ!

Scripture for further study

I SAMUEL 2:3, PSALM 139:1–6, PROVERBS 1:7, PROVERBS 3:19–20, ISAIAH 55:8–9, ROMANS 11:33–36, COLOSSIANS 2:3, I JOHN 3:20

EL-KANNA

A name can reveal a lot about a person. Throughout the Bible, we see men and women who are given names that become significant to their stories. In the Old Testament, Abram, whose name means "exalted father," is given a new name by God. God changes Abram's name to Abraham, which means "father of a multitude" and reflects God's covenantal relationship with Abraham and His promise to bless the nations through him (Genesis 17:5). Names or titles can also communicate one person's position in relation to others. For example, the Queen of England responds when called two important but very different titles: "Your Majesty" and "Granny." The latter specifies one's distinct relationship to the Queen, a special and intimate relationship that cannot be conveyed by her royal title alone. Names and titles hold meaning and embody relationships. The names of God help us see His glorious character shining brightly through the various ways He relates to His people.

In Hebrew, the name El-Kanna means "jealous God." We first see God use this name to refer to Himself when giving Moses the Ten Commandments as He says, "I, the Lord your God, am a jealous God" (Exodus 20:5). Extracting the meaning of this name of God means separating it from our human understanding of jealousy. We often think of it as akin to envy—wanting what we cannot have, which leads to insecurity and discontentment. In this way, jealousy is something we actively avoid. So what does it mean that our God is a jealous God?

When God describes Himself as jealous, it means that He is fiercely protective over what belongs to Him alone. God is wholly consumed with His glory and jealous for our worship. The use of El-Kanna in Scripture is inextricably linked to His warnings

God's jealousy reflects His holiness as He denounces our allegiance to lesser loves.

against idolatry and false worship. God established a covenant relationship with the people of Israel. They became His people, and He became their God (Exodus 6:7). God brought them out of Egypt to be His inheritance (Deuteronomy 4:20). God's people did not belong to Egypt. They did not belong to idols. They belonged to God and God alone. For Israel to worship other gods was to be unfaithful to their covenantal bond with God.

As we dwell on El-Kanna, this godly jealousy brings the character of God sharply into focus. God's jealousy reflects His holiness as He denounces our allegiance to lesser loves. God has no rival, for He alone is worthy of our praise. Being a jealous God does not mean that He is insecure or lacking. God's self-existence reminds us He needs nothing outside of Himself. God desires good for His children and becomes fiercely protective when they step off the path of obedience and into sin. He is jealous for our worship that belongs to Him alone.

Though we are recipients of this great love and providential care, our hearts are still prone to wander from God. We must continually fight the temptation to elevate the value of created things over the Creator. El-Kanna invites us to live an abundant life as we walk in holiness. We worship a God who is fiercely protective of us. El-Kanna. God is jealous for you. Give Him your whole life, for He is worthy.

Scripture for further study

EXODUS 20:5, EXODUS 34:14, DEUTERONOMY 4:20–24

EL-ROI

In a world where our lives can be on full display through social media, ironically, many of us have never felt more alone, desperate, and unseen. The face we give to the world is a mere facade of the spiritual and emotional people we are on the inside. We show people what we want them to see and yet wish they knew the "real" us. At the end of the day, no matter how many likes or shares we receive, we still feel unseen and unknown.

We are not the first ones to feel this way. In Genesis 16, Sarai, the long-barren wife of Abram, gave her Egyptian servant Hagar to Abram in order to provide him with an heir. Hagar conceived, and despite the fact it had been Sarai's idea, Sarai began to deal harshly with her. Hagar fled into the wilderness—likely feeling alone, abandoned, and forgotten—until the angel of the Lord found her. The angel of the Lord told her to return to her mistress and submit. He also promised her offspring would be multiplied, and she would bear a son named Ishmael. Hagar said to the Lord in Genesis 16:13, "You are El-roi . . . In this place, have I actually seen the one who sees me?"

Even in her lowly and cast-off position, God saw Hagar. He cared about her and her child. He cared about the despair and abandonment she felt. God saw Hagar for who she really was, blessed her with a promise of her own, and protected her from the contempt of her master. Even on our darkest days, God sees us and meets us right where we are. When your heart is breaking over the way you were treated, or when the hole you tried to fill with something other than God feels ten times bigger, God sees you. God knows the very number of hairs on your head (Luke 12:7).

*Even on our darkest days,
God sees us and meets
us right where we are.*

He knit you together in your mother's womb (Psalm 139:13). There is nothing too big for Him to handle and no small thing He does not see (Proverbs 15:3).

God's promise to Hagar is one of many in a very long list of promises He has kept. This seemingly unknown Egyptian servant was thrust into the grand narrative of Scripture as her child became the father of his own nation. Even on her darkest day, God saw her and did not leave her alone in her pain or despair. He does not leave us alone either. God sees the hole in each of our hearts that only He can fill. His divine plan from the beginning was to send Jesus to fill that hole. Whatever you may be facing, Jesus sees you, Jesus died for you, Jesus redeems you, and one day, you will dwell with Jesus forever in the new heaven and new earth.

On those days when you feel forgotten or like no one knows the real you, remember that the God who made you understands you better than anyone. God created every part of you. God sees you more clearly than you see yourself. If you find yourself feeling alone, remember the words of Deuteronomy 31:8, which say, "The Lord is the one who will go before you. He will be with you; he will not leave you or abandon you. Do not be afraid or discouraged." You can praise Him, for He is El-Roi—the God who sees you.

Scripture for further study
GENESIS 16, PSALM 139

ELOHIM

The word *elohim* is used in the Hebrew Bible more than 2,500 times. Although its meaning is not known for certain, it is widely thought that the root word *el* has connotations of power or might. Interestingly, though it is a name of God, the word *elohim* does not always refer to God. *El* was a common term among many nations and cultures for deity, and *elohim* is the masculine plural form of *el*. In the Bible, *elohim* sometimes refers to foreign gods (Exodus 12:12, Joshua 24:20), heavenly beings other than God such as angels and demons (Job 1:6), or, rarely, people with power and authority (Exodus 21:6, 1 Samuel 2:25 KJV). But the one true Elohim is God and God alone. There are many beings and people with power and authority in the Bible, yet

God stands alone as the One who creates all other beings and is the authoritative power over all.

Elohim is the very first name used for God in Genesis 1:1. In fact, it is the only name used for God between Genesis 1:1–2:3. Genesis 1:1 reads, "In the beginning, God created the heavens and the earth," or if we want to see this name of God in action, we can read it as "In the beginning, Elohim created the heavens and the earth." The Hebrew word used for "created" in this verse helps us define Elohim because creating is what Elohim does. The Hebrew word for "created" used here is *bārā'*. *Bārā'* means "to create from nothing." Elohim not only formed the heavens and the earth, but He spoke into existence the matter He used to form it. Psalm 33:6 says, "The heavens were made by the word of the Lord, and all the stars, by the breath of his mouth." His word,

His breath, made what was not yet appear. Humans can create, but they cannot *bārā'*. Only Elohim can *bārā'*. Our God is unique in that only He can form a creation out of nothing.

Creating something from nothing means creating something entirely new. Elohim does this repeatedly in the creation story. But He also does this in His relationships with people. In Exodus 34, God has strengthened Moses to lead His people from slavery in Egypt to freedom. God gives Moses the Ten Commandments on new stone tablets and renews His covenant and promise with His people. Exodus 34:10 says, "And the Lord responded: 'Look, I am making a covenant. In the presence of all your people I will perform wonders that have never been done in the whole earth or in any nation. All the people you live among will see the Lord's work, for what I am doing with you is awe-inspiring." God, Elohim, is promising to create something special between Him and His people. He will lead them, guide them, remain faithful to them, and be their God.

Then, in Psalm 51, we see that Elohim does yet another type of creating. David, who has sinned grievously against God, cries out for God to create in him a clean heart and renew a steadfast spirit within him (Psalm 51:10). David is asking Elohim to restore, renew, and redeem his sinful heart. Elohim has mercy on David, and although David struggles with sin for the rest of his life, he is also counted as a man who was after God's own heart (1 Samuel 13:14).

Only Elohim can restore a sinful heart.

Elohim is the creator of the heavens, the earth, all beings, and all things. Elohim is the initiator of His relationship with His people. He is the One who can renew what has been broken by sin. Elohim makes new things and makes things new again.

Everything and everyone has their beginning in God alone. He alone is Elohim.

Scripture for further study

GENESIS 1:1, PSALM 29:1, PSALM 53, PSALM 82:1, PSALM 89:7

ETERNAL SPIRIT

One of the Bible's greatest mysteries is the Trinity: God the Father, God the Son, and God the Holy Spirit. The Trinity is not explicitly explained anywhere in Scripture, but passage after passage points to the work of all three members of the Trinity in creating, saving, and sustaining life. The Trinity is one God in three persons. Though many books have been written about this awesome phenomenon, what we must remember is that our finite brains cannot fully understand the infinite mind of God. But we can trust who He says He is because of His faithfulness from generation to generation.

One name for the triune God in Scripture is Eternal Spirit." The word "eternal" means "endless, existing at all times." This aspect of God's character is seen as early as Genesis 1:2, which says, "the Spirit of God was hovering over the surface of the waters." The Eternal Spirit was actively involved in the creation of the universe. The Eternal Spirit also rested on those God called throughout the Old Testament. For example, the Spirit was with Abraham as he fathered God's chosen nation, with Moses when through the Spirit he parted the Red Sea, and with Joshua as he led the Israelites into the Promised Land. The Spirit guided these men and used them to shepherd His ultimate plan of redemption for His people.

Though more subtle in the Old Testament, the Eternal Spirit has a more prominent role in the New Testament. Specifically, the Eternal Spirit is mentioned in Hebrews 9:14 when the author asks, "how much more will the blood of Christ, who through the eternal Spirit offered himself without blemish to God, cleanse our consciences from dead works so that we can serve the living God?" All three members of the Trinity are present in this verse.

The Father, Son, and Spirit each work to provide salvation for mankind. One of the Eternal Spirit's greatest roles was to present Jesus to the Father as a worthy sacrifice. When God accepted that sacrifice—and when we, in turn, accept the forgiveness provided by Christ's atonement on our behalf—

the Spirit fills our hearts and helps us serve the Father.

God, the Eternal Spirit, rained down on the believers at Pentecost, just as Jesus had promised (John 14:16–17, Acts 2). The Spirit fills the hearts of those who seek forgiveness from their sin, trust in the sacrificial death of Christ, and seek to live their lives for the Lord.

The Eternal Spirit dwells within each believer, taking us from death to life.

Though only used once in the Bible in Hebrews 9:14, this name illustrates God's character as displayed across the pages of Scripture. The prophet Samuel tells us, "Furthermore, the Eternal One of Israel does not lie or change his mind, for he is not man who changes his mind" (1 Samuel 15:29). Likewise, the Apostle Paul reminds us, "Now to the King eternal, immortal, invisible, the only God, be honor and glory forever and ever. Amen" (1 Timothy 1:17). God is not like man. He is eternal, immortal, and invisible. His Spirit works on His behalf to draw sinners to Christ for salvation, to aid believers in their walk toward holiness, and to take each believer before the throne of God at the end of their life.

The Eternal Spirit fills us with all the fullness of God through Christ Jesus (Ephesians 3:19).

Scripture for further study

JOHN 16:5–15, ACTS 2, HEBREWS 9:11–28

EVERLASTING

God is the Everlasting God. He is El Olam. While *el*, as we learned on page 85, was a common name for a deity, the Hebrew root word for *'olām* refers to the infiniteness of time. It was common for people to wish *'olām* upon kings and rulers as a sign of respect and honor. We see this in places like 1 Kings 1:31, where Bathsheba honored King David in his last days by saying, "May my lord King David live forever!" However, when the Hebrew word *'olām* is prescribed to God as an attribute, it takes on a new meaning. Of course, no earthly king will live and reign forever, but God will. And not only is He without end, but He is also without beginning. God is everlasting. He has no beginning and no end. He exists outside of the limits of time and space. There has never been a moment when He did not exist—ever. God's infiniteness makes Him the one and only being through whom all people of all time have been created and sustained.

We find claims regarding God's infiniteness throughout Scripture. In Psalm 90:1–2, Moses calls God the refuge of every generation. God was there before the mountains were born; He gave birth to the earth and the world. If mankind has found comfort, refuge, joy, or delight in any created thing, it is only because the uncreated and everlasting God has created it. In contrast, Psalm 90:3–4 describes the finiteness of mankind. Every person lives but for a brief moment in light of the Everlasting God. People are like grass that springs up, sprouts and grows, and then withers and dies. Human beings come from dust and return to dust. We live for a moment, but God exists in His fullness always and forever.

This begs the question: if mankind exists for such a brief moment, why would the Everlasting God spend His time and attention on

God is everlasting. He has no beginning and no end. He exists outside of the limits of time and space.

them? He does this because He has made an everlasting covenant with His people (Hebrews 13:20). He has promised to be a close and personal God to those who belong to Him for all time. He has promised to invite them into His everlasting kingdom (Psalm 145:13) and give them eternal life (John 3:16). When finite men trust in an infinite God for their salvation from sin, they receive the gift of being with Him for all eternity.

God also possesses everlasting power and strength. Isaiah 40:28 says He never becomes faint or weary, and there is no limit to His understanding. Mankind has many limits. Our bodies require physical, mental, and emotional rest. We stumble and fall (Isaiah 40:29–30). But those who trust in the Everlasting God will be renewed by His infinite reserves. God gives those who depend on Him new strength, so they can continue without faltering.

God has no limits. He has always been and always will be. He is not restrained by time or space. He never becomes depleted or fatigued. And incredibly, He invites small, finite men to believe in Him and receive everlasting life. His love and grace are as boundless as His existence. He is El Olam—the Everlasting God.

Scripture for further study

GENESIS 9:16, GENESIS 21:33, 2 SAMUEL 7:13,
PSALM 90:2, ISAIAH 40:28, HEBREWS 13:20

FIRST AND LAST

In our world today, whoever is first has the power. If someone wins a race, it is typically because of strength and skill. Yet God refers to Himself as the First and Last. God's identity as the First and Last communicates His eternality and superiority, which refers to the truth that God is before, behind, and above all things. In Isaiah 44:6, God says, "I am the first and I am the last. There is no God but me." God demonstrates His superiority by revealing the futility of idols throughout Isaiah 44. He describes how the idols that humans create with their hands always fall short. The futility of idols reveals the supremacy of God. God stands alone. Nothing and no one compares to His greatness. There is no God but Him.

However, mankind often treats God as if He is not the First and Last. God told the Israelites that there is no God but Him, but still, they turned away from Him to worship false Gods. The Israelites placed idols as their objects of worship instead of God. Sadly, today is no different. Mankind still rebels against God and refuses to worship Him. Many people see money, relationships, and success as their ultimate value and means of satisfaction. But, when money runs out, relationships fail, and success falters, these people are brought to despair.

Even those of us who are followers of Jesus can struggle to worship God wholeheartedly. We can delight in the things of this world more than we delight in God. We can value the attention and opinions of others over how God sees us. We can base our happiness on the amount of money in our bank accounts or the beauty of our homes. But, when whatever it is we delight in fails us, we are reminded once again of the eternality and supremacy of God. The things of this world will falter, break, and crumble—but God always remains.

The things of this world will falter, break, and crumble—but God always remains.

The truth that God is the First and Last reminds us to put God first instead of last. When we put God first in our lives, we value and worship Him above all else. Putting God first sets the Lord in His rightful place—on the throne of our hearts. But, to place God first, we must remove the idols that often prevent Him from being first. While this does not mean we do away with money, people, or possessions completely, it does involve prioritizing God above these things and placing our identity in Him alone.

Keeping God as our first love can be a struggle, but that is why we have Jesus. The triune nature of God means that Jesus, too, shares this name of God. Jesus says in Revelation 1:17–18, "Don't be afraid. I am the First and the Last, and the Living One. I was dead, but look—I am alive forever and ever, and I hold the keys of death and Hades." The supremacy of God is revealed in this passage as Jesus declares His power over death. The same power Jesus had to conquer death is the same power that lives in us. Through the Holy Spirit, we are given the ability to fight against the temptation to worship anything other than God. We receive the conviction and the strength to reorder our loves to put God first again. In the moments we feel our worship of God slipping, we can rest in the power of the Spirit and remind ourselves that God is the First and Last. There is no one like God, so let us worship Him alone.

Scripture for further study

ISAIAH 41:4, REVELATION 22:13

FORTRESS

Have you ever visited the site of an old battleground? Historic battlegrounds often have a fort that soldiers used as their means of protection. Soldiers would depend on these forts to defend and shelter them from the enemy. These buildings often boast tall and powerful walls of stone. However, even the strongest forts do not remain eternally sturdy and safe. The walls may be destroyed by agents of warfare or deteriorated by natural elements. Although an old fort may remain standing to some extent, it is likely not the strong defense it once was.

In the Bible, God is called a Fortress. David writes in Psalm 18:2, "The Lord is my rock, my fortress, and my deliverer, my God, my rock where I seek refuge." Like a fort or fortress, God is a source of protection. But unlike the fortresses humans make, God is a fortress who remains strong. God is an all-powerful God. Nothing and no one can weaken or destroy Him. The indestructibility of God means that God is a place of constant and complete refuge. Whenever we are afraid, we can run to God and rest in His presence. In Him, we find the strength we need to withstand the wars of hardship and fear. But do we always go to God in moments of fear or trouble? At times, we can run to other people and places for refuge and comfort, but these people and places cannot deliver us consistent refuge. They may provide some relief, but they are not designed to give us perpetual refuge and security.

God is our one true source of refuge. He alone can provide us with the strength, comfort, and shelter we need in moments of fear. As our Fortress, God is dependable and reliable. Therefore, we can trust Him. Even if our circumstances do not change or hardships continue, we can remain firm as we trust the Lord.

As our Fortress, God is dependable and reliable. Therefore, we can trust Him.

We can also have hope in moments of terror and trouble because of our relationship with Jesus. The forgiveness we receive from Christ rescues us from the enemy's grip and gives us eternal security. Although we are not promised complete protection from trouble, because of our salvation, we are promised that our eternal life is secure in Christ's hands. No matter what happens in this life, we have the sure promise of deliverance from death. We are forever safe.

God is our eternal and indestructible Fortress. Therefore, let us not depend on anything else to give us the security that God can. Let us not run to anything else in times of fear or trouble but the Lord. When the world feels heavy, run to Him. When your pain feels unbearable, run to Him. When the suffering does not lift, run to Him. When anxieties press down, run to Him. In any and every situation, you can come to God and declare to Him, "My refuge and my fortress, my God, in whom I trust" (Psalm 91:2 ESV).

Scripture for further study

PSALM 144:1–2

GOOD SHEPHERD

Humans tend to pursue autonomy, valuing the ability to make our own rules or decisions in life. In our sin, we are like feral horses who buck any efforts to tame our wild hearts. We ignore, run away from, and resist God's law. Though our nature is fallen, we are still image-bearers. In other words, though our flesh is rebellious, deep down, we long for guidance. We yearn for someone to care for us and walk before us as we navigate unknown or dark places. We want something to focus on when we do not know where we are headed in life. This is our truest desire because God originally intended for us to be like His sheep. He designed us to see Him as our Shepherd. But, because of our sin, we do not have the ability to give up our pursuit of autonomy and follow the Lord on our own.

Yet, while we were sinners, God continued to see us as His sheep, and He promised to save us. When the prophet Isaiah predicted that the Israelites, who were God's chosen nation, would be led away in captivity due to their sin, he also added that the Lord would remain faithful to His character. Isaiah said, "He protects his flock like a shepherd; he gathers the lambs in his arms and carries them in the fold of his garment. He gently leads those that are nursing" (Isaiah 40:11). God would rescue His people from harm because He would take them into His possession. At the same time, the Word of the Lord also predicted that a Man would come to be Shepherd for God's people, tending their greatest need (Ezekiel 34:23).

The coming of Jesus Christ fulfilled these promises. Jesus called Himself the Good Shepherd (John 10:11–17). In this name, Jesus claimed to be God in human form. He claimed to be the Savior sent from heaven to lead the Lord's sheep out of chaos. And

We are His sheep, and He is our Shepherd. Come under His care, and follow His staff for eternity.

by His saving work, Jesus proved to be the true overseer of our souls. Showing a sheep-like demeanor, Jesus lived meekly and always looked to the Father for guidance. When He endured trying times, like the wilderness temptation, He clung to the Father's Word. He kept His eye on the goodness of God to give Him peace. And as Shepherd, Jesus extended goodness and peace to others. He healed the weak and cared for the lost. He pointed to Himself for the way out of evil's grasp. When Jesus died and rose from the grave, He completed the work necessary to tend to our greatest need: freedom from sin.

With the impact of His saving work applied by the Holy Spirit, Jesus transforms our nature from unruly to dependent. He gives us a new passion: a desire to walk near the Lord's staff. We should never want to depart from the grace of God. We are His sheep, and He is our Shepherd. Come under His care, and follow His staff for eternity.

Scripture for further study

PSALM 23:1-3, ISAIAH 40:11, EZEKIEL 34:23, MATTHEW 9:36, JOHN 10:11-17, REVELATION 7:17

GREAT HIGH PRIEST

In the beginning, mankind freely walked in the Lord's presence. In the garden of Eden, Adam and Eve experienced intimacy with their Maker and enjoyed the blessing of His nearness. But unfortunately, the first humans exchanged their satisfaction in God for the passions of their flesh. They disobeyed God's Word by eating from the forbidden tree. In their sin, Adam and Eve demonstrated the desire to be apart from the Lord, and because of their rebellion, they could no longer be in the Lord's presence. God demanded a holy place and a holy people. Adam and Eve were now corrupt and would be consumed in the Lord's sight, so God expelled them from the garden. He honored their decision to be separate from His nearness and gave them over to the destruction they desired.

Sin created a chasm between the Lord and us, as well. This separation is a problem for all of humanity. God designed us to be with Him, but our sinful hearts run from His love. Still expelled from the garden, we cannot intimately walk with God like Adam first did. We cannot stand before God's holy throne. But God has been merciful. Though we deserved alienation, God devised a plan so that we could be in His midst again.

We see a shadow of this plan through the Old Testament priests. God organized a select group of men for this role. Their completed duties were essential to ensure that the presence of the Lord abided with the Israelites. They were to lead the people in obedience, teach them the Law, and intercede for them in the temple and tabernacle. The priests also paid for sins through animal sacrifice. The high priest was unique in his role because, once a year, he was the only one allowed to enter the Holy of Holies, the most sacred part of the temple and tabernacle. There, the

The Old Testament high priest ultimately pointed to the Great High Priest, Jesus Christ.

glory of God dwelled, surrounded by materials that resembled a heavenly garden. At this time, the high priest paid for the entire community's sins for that year. He did so by sprinkling the blood of a sacrificed animal before God's altar.

The Old Testament high priest ultimately pointed to the Great High Priest, Jesus Christ, as the author of Hebrews named Him. The ones serving as high priests in the Old Testament were sinners who needed their debts paid before they could enter the Holy of Holies. But Jesus is a perfect representative. He played the part of pre-fallen Adam as He freely entered the intimacy of the garden. Jesus brought His sacrifice and shed His blood on the altar. He covered us with holiness. In His strength, Jesus closed the chasm between God and us, bringing us to the holy throne. Jesus continues to serve as our Great High Priest, interceding when we struggle with sin. Despite these struggles, we can know that Jesus is still for us. The power of His blood will not fail. Through faith in Christ, we are able to draw near to God without limits and experience His satisfaction forever.

Scripture for further study

HEBREWS 4:14–16, HEBREWS 5:1–10, HEBREWS 7:11–28

HIDING PLACE

A good hiding place can provide quiet safety, a refuge from the chaos outside. As children, we played games like hide-and-seek and peekaboo. The best part was waiting in anticipation of being found, shrieking with laughter upon hearing the words, "There you are! I found you." But as the years pass and we get older, it seems we often get less happy about being found. Perhaps it is because, as adults, we have very different reasons for hiding. We sneak away to the bathroom just to get a few minutes alone. We have days that are so bad we just want to get back in bed and hide from the world. In our shame, we attempt to hide our sin from others or from God. The more we hide, the less we want to be found.

David understood the instinct to hide. Not only did he physically hide in caves to preserve his own life, but David also tried to hide his sin from God and others. In 2 Samuel 11–12, we find the story of David and Bathsheba. After sleeping with Bathsheba and later discovering she was pregnant, David schemed to kill her husband Uriah under the pretense of battle so that he could take Bathsheba as his wife. When Nathan exposed David and confronted him over this grievous sin, David repented before Nathan and before the Lord, no longer able to hide.

We all want to hide from time to time. Hiding presumes safety, but this depends on where we hide. The book of Psalms points us to God as our Hiding Place, our refuge in times of trouble. David seemed to know this better than anyone as he penned roughly half of the psalms in the Bible. In Psalm 32:7, he writes, "You are my hiding place; you protect me from trouble. You surround me with joyful shouts of deliverance." David also says of God, "For he will hide me in his shelter in the day of trou-

Resting in God as our Hiding Place means we can cease striving to find comfort apart from Him.

ble; he will conceal me under the cover of his tent; he will lift me high upon a rock" (Psalm 27:5 ESV). After David's failed attempts to run and hide, he trusted in God and found rest in Him as his Hiding Place. David knew that God was the only One strong enough to protect him.

The world entices us to seek shelter in temporary things. Our physical beauty, our earthly relationships, our worldly possessions—these things cannot and will not provide lasting refuge. When we seek comfort in the world, we are like the baby playing peekaboo, covering our eyes, thinking that we cannot be seen. But in reality, we are hiding in plain sight. Resting in God as our Hiding Place means we can cease striving to find comfort apart from Him. God will give us rest in the weariest parts of our souls. This does not mean that we are guaranteed a life free of pain or suffering. The psalms serve as a reminder that we will encounter difficult times, but we can seek shelter in the One who holds our eternity in His hands. He is the one Hiding Place that no one can take from us. We cannot be snatched out of His sovereign hand (John 10:28). Even on our worst days, we can find refuge in the Lord Jesus Christ. When He is our Hiding Place, nothing can separate us. We are secure in Him.

Scripture for further study

PSALM 61, PSALM 119:114, ISAIAH 28:17, ISAIAH 32:1–8

HOLY ONE

Holiness is at the center of who God is.

God's holiness sets Him apart as supreme over all creation. He is distinctly different from every other being, including us. When God delivered His people out of Egypt and through the parted Red Sea, they rejoiced, singing, "Lord, who is like you among the gods? Who is like you, glorious in holiness, revered with praises, performing wonders?" (Exodus 15:11). Everything He is and everything He does is intrinsically holy.

The prophet Isaiah had an intimate experience with God's holiness. In Isaiah 6, he saw the Lord in a vision—the King seated on His throne with robes so majestic that they filled the temple. Angels surrounding the King could not help but proclaim, "Holy, holy, holy is the Lord of Armies" (Isaiah 6:3). No king compares to Him. Isaiah responded with awareness of his own sin as well as the sinfulness of God's people: "Woe is me for I am ruined because I am a man of unclean lips and live among a people of unclean lips, and because my eyes have seen the King, the Lord of Armies" (Isaiah 6:5).

It is no wonder that Isaiah referred to God as the Holy One of Israel throughout his book. This name is repeated over twenty times as Isaiah reminds God's people of His character and His personal relationship with Israel. The people rebelled against God's holiness by conducting themselves in unholy ways, doing what was right in their own eyes. As Isaiah exposed the wickedness of Israel's actions, he continually called them back to God, the Holy One of Israel, the One who led them out of Egypt and through the Red Sea. The glory of God's holiness on display compelled Isaiah to proclaim God's message to His chosen yet rebellious people, to plead with them to turn back to the Lord, the Holy One of Israel (Isaiah 10:20).

Jesus Christ is the Holy One of God, perfectly loving and righteous, without spot or blemish (1 Peter 1:19). During His earthly ministry, Jesus was acknowledged as the Holy One by two very different sources—a demon and a disciple. In Mark 1:24, Jesus rebuked and cast out an unclean spirit who cried, "What do you have to do with us, Jesus of Nazareth? Have you come to destroy us? I know who you are—the Holy One of God!" The unholy spirit was in the presence of a holy God, and the witnesses were in awe of Jesus's authority over the unseen world. In John 6:68–69, the disciples believed Jesus held the words of eternal life, and Peter proclaimed Jesus as the Holy One of God.

> *Even in the midst of opposition and persecution, the deity of Jesus is displayed for the world to see.*

God's holiness is the standard by which we are judged. No matter how hard we try, we will never meet God's standard of holiness in our own strength. It is not enough to merely believe in God, for even demons believe and shudder (James 2:19). The Bible tells us that our sin against a perfect God deserves death (Romans 6:23). And yet, Jesus Christ, the Holy One, laid down His perfect life and died the death we deserved. This is the upside-down kingdom of God. Jesus, the King of kings, is lowly and humble in heart (Matthew 11:29). He knew no sin and yet became sin for us so that we could be made righteous before Him (2 Corinthians 5:21). The Holy One draws the unholy to Himself, cleansed by the precious blood of Christ. As those who believe in Him, we will be in the presence of the Holy One now and forever.

Scripture for further study

PSALM 89, PROVERBS 9:10, ISAIAH 6, ISAIAH 41:8–14

God existed before the beginning of time. He always was. This is one of those profound mysteries that our finite minds cannot fully comprehend on this side of heaven. He is the eternal, uncreated One whose very nature is not defined by anything other than Himself. In Exodus 3, Moses has an astonishing encounter with this God in a burning bush that, though it is on fire, is not being consumed. Not only that, but Moses also hears a voice calling out his name. God reveals Himself as the voice, establishing His identity to Moses as "the God of your father, the God of Abraham, the God of Isaac, and the God of Jacob" (Exodus 3:6). God has seen the oppression of His people and knows their pain intimately. God tells Moses that He will accomplish His purposes through Moses as he leads God's people out of Egypt and into freedom.

Naturally, Moses has some questions. First, Moses questions his own ability as someone chosen by God to come up against a powerful foe such as Pharaoh. In verse 11, he asks, "Who am I that I should go to Pharaoh and that I should bring the Israelites out of Egypt?" In Moses's disbelief, God responds graciously—not by affirming Moses's ability or strength for such a task but by pointing back to Himself and His unchanging character. God promises that He will be present with Moses, just as He has been with His people from the very beginning.

Moses moves from "Who am *I*?" to "Who are *You*?" by asking God for His name in case the Israelites ask. There were many gods in the time of the Israelites, so how would Moses distinguish this God from the others? Then God replied to Moses, "I AM WHO I AM. This is what you are to say to the Israelites: I AM has sent me to you" (Exodus 3:14). Names through-

Just as the Great I AM was present with Moses at the burning bush, God is present with us today.

out the Bible have great significance, especially if it is a name of God handed down from God Himself. I AM means He is God because He is God. He exists because He exists. He will be because He will be. This encompasses His complete and eternal state of being in the past, present, and future. God has dominion and authority over all of time and creation, yet He is intimately involved in the present lives of His people.

We encounter another questioning of God's identity in the gospel of John: "Who do you claim to be?" (John 8:53). When this was asked of Jesus, He replied, "Truly I tell you, before Abraham was, I am" (John 8:58). The use of the phrase "I AM" elicited such a strong response from the crowd. They picked up stones to throw as they believed that Jesus must be stoned to death for such a blasphemous statement. How could this man claim to be the God of Abraham, the same God who revealed Himself to Moses in the burning bush? They failed to recognize that their long-awaited Messiah, God incarnate, was before them. He was the Word made flesh, and He dwelt among His people (John 1:14). Just as the Great I AM was present with Moses at the burning bush, God is present with us today. We can worship Him as the eternal, self-existent God, who is the same now and forever.

Scripture for further study

EXODUS 3, PSALM 90:2, JOHN 8:48–59, REVELATION 1:8

IMMANUEL

God's people waited in silence for four hundred years. These centuries, known as the intertestamental period, spanned between the events of the Old and New Testaments. During this time, God did not send any prophets or messages to His people. From generation to generation, the Israelites waited, wondering if God would remain faithful. They clung to their God's past promises and to the hope that He would fulfill them through a Messiah. But still, the questions remained: *How long would they have to wait? Would He ever speak to them again? Would God remain faithful to His promises?*

The New Testament opens with the Gospel account of Matthew, which details the birth of Jesus Christ, the coming Messiah. Half of the first chapter of Matthew is dedicated to the genealogy of Jesus. This may seem like a long-winded way of introducing Jesus's story until we think back to Matthew's original audience — the people of God, who were waiting and praying during those quiet years. In Matthew 1:18–25, Joseph discovers his soon-to-be bride, Mary, is pregnant. He finds himself in a predicament. Knowing the baby is not his, what is he going to do? Instead of exposing her supposed sin of adultery to the world, Joseph decides to leave her quietly. But that night, an angel of the Lord comes to Joseph in a dream, telling him what Mary already knew — she would give birth to a Son who would take away the sins of His people, the One for whom God's people had been anticipating and waiting. The Lord had spoken after years of silence, and His people were listening.

After silence, a burst of hope. The wait was over. God had not abandoned His people. In fact, He was coming to dwell among them, to redeem them from their sin. Joseph kept Mary as his wife. His obedience was not deterred by his complicated circum-

Take great comfort today in the truth that no matter what you face in this life, God is with you.

stances. This opening genealogy soothes the weary, worrying hearts of God's people as they remember the words of Isaiah: "Therefore, the Lord himself will give you a sign: See, the virgin will conceive, have a son, and name him Immanuel" (Isaiah 7:14). In Matthew's genealogy, each name leads to another and to another until it ends with the name of Jesus—the Messiah who would break through their world as a baby. This genealogy serves as a reminder that God is faithful. He keeps His promises. He is Immanuel, which means He is God with us.

In the midst of our own circumstances, we can often forget that God is with us. Like the Israelites, we can wonder about God's faithfulness and doubt His timing. The Bible is one story of God's continual faithfulness to His people, even when they are faithless. Jesus came to redeem us from our sins and reconcile us to Himself. He is with us always and will never abandon us (Deuteronomy 31:8). When we are lonely, we can cry out to Immanuel—God is with us. When we rejoice, God is with us. When we mourn, God is with us. Take great comfort today in the truth that no matter what you face in this life, God is with you.

Scripture for further study
ISAIAH 7:14, MATTHEW 1:23

JEHOVAH-JIREH

A wide-eyed preacher shouts the prosperity gospel over his congregation. He distorts the Lord's name, Jehovah-Jireh, which means "the Lord will provide." Speaking to poor congregants, the preacher promises God will provide for their financial needs — if only they will have more faith.

But the reality is that God does not promise to give us financial comfort based on the amount of belief we demonstrate. According to God's good will, He gives material wealth to some and poverty to others, as 1 Samuel 2:7 states. God has ordained both life circumstances as opportunities to mature us in Christ and reflect the gospel. James 1:9–10 says, "Let the brother of humble circumstances boast in his exaltation, but let the rich boast in his humiliation because he will pass away like a flower of the field." This truth does not mean we should not pray for financial relief or have faith that God can bring us out of economic strain. We should still do so, but we should also show utmost gratitude to our God, Jehovah-Jireh, for already bringing us out of spiritual poverty, forgiving our moral debts, and providing salvation.

In the context of Scripture, this name is seen in Genesis 22. God tested Abraham, a man to whom God promised to make his family into a great nation. God told Abraham to go to a mountain and sacrifice his son Isaac there. Abraham was obedient, having faith that God would either provide a lamb for the offering or bring Isaac back to life (Genesis 22:8, Hebrews 11:19). As Abraham took out the knife to strike Isaac, the angel of the Lord stopped him. Abraham looked up and saw a ram caught in a bush. God provided the sacrifice to forgive their sins. Because of His provision, Abraham called that place on the mountain Jehovah-Jireh, which translated to English from the original Hebrew means "The Lord Will Provide" (Genesis 22:14).

When all material wealth and comforts fade, the gifts of Christ will never cease or perish.

This moment foreshadows the saving work of Jesus. Through Jesus, God provided the salvation He promised. The Son of God was led to a mountain place and hung on a cross. He died there, willingly offering His body up as a sacrifice. He was the perfect Lamb who took away our sins. In return, Jesus gave us eternal life.

If He provided salvation—our greatest spiritual need—then surely Jehovah-Jireh will provide us with abundance. This abundance will ultimately manifest when we see the glory of God completely in eternity. Our rich inheritance will be found in His fullness. But even now, Jehovah-Jireh gives us everything we need. Most of all, however, Jehovah-Jireh gives us His presence, which is more valuable than all the money in the world.

When bills mount, when we are drowning in debt, or when we are unsure how to get food on the table, we can ask the Provider to intervene. We can pray with content hearts that have joy in the Lord's presence now and hope in a heavenly abundance in the future. We can do this confidently because when all material wealth and comforts fade, the gifts of Christ will never cease or perish. Our God desires to provide us with a rich, everlasting grace.

Scripture for further study
GENESIS 22:1–19, PHILIPPIANS 4:19, ROMANS 8:32

JEHOVAH-NISSI

In Exodus 17:8, the Amalekites, an enemy nation, came and attacked the desert-dwelling Israelites. Moses commanded Joshua to take some men to fight against their attackers and said He would stand atop a hill, holding God's staff in his hands. This staff was given to Moses by God. God used it to do many miraculous things, such as turning all of the rivers and water in Egypt into blood and parting the Red Sea to provide the Israelites with a way of escape from Egypt. The staff was used to show God's power to Pharaoh so that Pharaoh would come to fear God and free God's people from slavery.

In battle, the staff represented that same power of God, but it was also a practical tool for battle-worn men. It was typical in the ancient middle east to raise a banner in battle. This banner would be visible to every man fighting the war. The banner was a place the wounded could come for care. It was a place to gather, strategize, and regroup. And it proudly displayed the symbol of the king or kingdom on behalf of whom the warriors were fighting. Moses did not display a banner during the battle with the Amalekites but rather held up the staff of God. This staff represented God's power and presence with the Israelites.

During this battle, whenever Moses held the staff in the air, the Israelites advanced against the Amalekites. But whenever his arms wearied and he lowered the staff, the Amalekites gained ground against the Israelites. The battle waged on, and Moses tired. So, a stone was placed under him so that he could sit, and Aaron and Hur held Moses's arms high until the Israelites emerged victoriously.

After this miraculous victory, Moses built an altar to the Lord and named it Jehovah-Nissi, which translated to English from the original Hebrew means "The Lord Is My Banner" (Exodus 17:15). Other nations had kings and kingdoms they valiantly fought to defend. But Israel fought for One much more glorious. They fought for God. God was the One who gave Israel its marching orders. They did not rely on human strategy but on a divine directive. God was the One who defined the cause for which Israel fought. The Israelites did not fight for personal glory but to accomplish the will of God, which sometimes involved removing excessively wicked people from the earth through war. And they did not fight in their own strength but with the power of God. God ensured Israel's victory by His might and for His glory.

All believers can say, as Moses did, "The Lord is my banner."

He is the One from whom we receive our direction. He is where we go when we are weary or wounded. When we look to Him, we are reminded that He is the purpose for which we live. He has promised to provide victory over sin and death for all who believe in Jesus. Our lives are meant to be rallied around who He is and the way He has asked us to live.

In Exodus 17:16, Moses lifted his hands to the Lord as he prayed at the altar he built. He confessed that it is only by the power of God that Israel will defeat her enemies from generation to generation. The battle was the Lord's—not Moses's. The banner of God invites us to surrender our lives before it, just as Moses did.

Our lives and the battles we face are not ours but the Lord's.

Therefore, we should raise our hands in submission to the Lord and allow Him to be our guide, our strength, and the driving purpose for our every move.

In the Lord, we find victory over our shame, sin, and shortcomings. We find direction, comfort, and purpose. God is our banner; He is our Jehovah-Nissi.

Scripture for further study

EXODUS 17:8–16, PSALM 20:5–8, PSALM 60:4, ISAIAH 62:10

JEHOVAH-RAPHA

When we take a moment to look at our world, it is easy to see the sickness and brokenness that abounds. Hospitals are full, doctor's offices have long waitlists, and counseling centers have never been busier. Sin has infected our bodies, minds, and hearts. It has taken its toll, and creation longs for healing and restoration (Romans 8:22–23). However, in His goodness and grace, God has given us hope through His name Jehovah-Rapha, which translated to English from the original Hebrew means "The Lord Who Heals."

The name Jehovah-Rapha first appears in Scripture in Exodus 15. Moses had led the Israelites out of bondage from Egypt, and they were moving across the desert toward the Promised Land. It was a hot, dry, and difficult journey with hardly any water supply. The Israelites grumbled and complained. Yet they were encouraged as they approached Marah, an oasis with many wells, until they realized the water was bitter and not good for drinking. Moses cried to the Lord in desperation, and God provided a solution to make the water sweet. Then, in verse 26, God said, "If you will carefully obey the Lord your God, do what is right in his sight, pay attention to his commands, and keep all his statutes, I will not inflict any illnesses on you that I inflicted on the Egyptians. For I am the Lord who heals you." These words, "the Lord who heals you," are a translation of the phrase Jehovah-Rapha."Through these words, God reveals Himself to be Jehovah-Rapha; He is the God who heals.

Even in their wilderness wanderings, God promised to heal their physical infirmities. He provided for their physical needs and kept them from the diseases that plagued other nations, such as Egypt.

In our broken world, we can trust that we still have a God who heals.

Jehovah-Rapha has performed miracle after miracle by healing cancer, neurological disorders, depression, and many other afflictions that plague His people. These physical healings are a gift and point to His power over all things—but

the healing we most crave is healing for our sinful souls.

Even if complete physical healing does not come in this lifetime, God provides complete healing for His children through Jesus Christ. Creation has longed for healing since the moment sin marred God's perfect creation. God brought healing to sinful hearts when Jesus willingly died on the cross and defeated sin and death through His resurrection. Jehovah-Rapha brought healing through His sacrifice so that by His wounds, we are healed (1 Peter 2:24). During His earthly ministry, Jesus healed multitudes from diseases and illnesses. But He never lost sight of the ultimate healing He was to provide through His sacrifice, which would heal the broken relationship between God and His image-bearers.

Whatever you may be facing physically, call on Jehovah-Rapha! He hears the cry of His children, and He desires to heal you. Sometimes, that healing will be physical healing on this side of heaven. Other times, the healing will come when you see Him face to face in eternity. While you await your physical healing, your soul can find healing in Him now. Jesus gave His life so that we can be reconciled to God. Our hearts are now washed clean and healed from sin, and we can approach His throne with boldness. Through Christ, God heals our unfaithfulness and calls us to Himself (Jeremiah 3:22).

Rest in the arms of your Healer, knowing your spiritual healing will bring eternal healing in the presence of Jehovah-Rapha.

Scripture for further study
ISAIAH 61:1, JAMES 5:13–16, 1 PETER 2:21–25

JEHOVAH-SHALOM

Our world is full of chaos. Destruction is present everywhere. Rulers topple. Wars break out. Gunshots fire, and bombs go off. Inhabitants live in fear and confusion. Screams deafen ears. In these dark moments, people may ask where God is. They may wonder if peace will ever come. How can broken pieces be put back together after such devastation? Where can souls find rest? These cries of the weary radiate from their hearts as they seek Jehovah-Shalom, the One who is able to restore.

The name Jehovah-Shalom is translated from the original Hebrew language to English as "The Lord Is Peace" (Judges 6:24). In the biblical sense, peace is more than the absence of conflict. The Hebrew word *šālôm*, or "shalom," refers to a feeling of wholeness, safety, and harmony. Biblical peace involves taking something that is broken and restoring it to its complete design. Shalom is used to describe the state of one's well-being. Have you ever felt like your inner person was missing something—as if your soul could not get to a place of calm and stability? Shalom addresses this feeling and brings deep peace. Shalom is also used to describe relationships. Due to sin, our relationships with God and others are fractured, but biblical peace brings reconciliation between parties.

Scripture indicates Jehovah-Shalom as a name of God in Judges 6. At this point in redemptive history, the Israelites were being oppressed by a pagan group called the Midianites. It was a time of chaos and destruction, and the Israelites cried out for help. Though the Israelites had committed evil in the land, they were still God's people. So the Lord raised up a man named Gideon to fight the Midianites in battle. Seeing that Gideon was afraid, God told him to have peace, for He would not let Gideon fall. Gideon

then built an altar and called the place Jehovah-Shalom—"The Lord is My Peace" (Judges 6:24). With the Lord's help, Gideon defeated the Midianites. However, though the conflict ceased, the Israelites still did not have true shalom. Sin continued to break God's people apart.

Gideon's military victory was a symbol of the peace that Jesus, centuries later, won. As the prophets predicted, Jesus embodied shalom. Because He was fully God, His inner person was one of soundness, strength, and tranquility. The kingdom of darkness did not shake Jesus. He remained secure and committed to accomplishing the Father's will. When Jesus finished His work on the cross, He conquered sin and freed us from its burdens. As a result, we are reconciled to the Father. Through our faith in Christ, the Holy Spirit replaces our broken identity with one that is whole in Jesus. As restored people of God, we are able to reconcile our relationships with others and reflect shalom in a fallen world.

Though there may be chaos and destruction around us, we can still live in a state of shalom. We do not have to be troubled, for salvation in Jesus is the thing that fills our most severe lack. Christ's grace makes us whole, and His love gives us rest. We can pray for the brokenness we encounter on this earth while always looking to the Prince of Peace, Jesus Christ (Isaiah 9:6).

Scripture for further study

JUDGES 6:11–24, ISAIAH 9:5–6, JOHN 14:27, JOHN 16:33, EPHESIANS 2:14, PHILIPPIANS 4:6–7

KING

What comes to your mind when you read the word "king"? Do you see a man on a throne with a crown? Or a vast and glorious kingdom? The word "king" points us to a ruler who has authority over a country. Throughout Scripture, God is referred to as King. But God is a different kind of King. God does not have authority over a country—He has authority over all the earth. Human kings typically inherit their throne through birth and hold their position until death. God, however, is an eternal God. He has always existed and will always exist. The world that He created is His domain forever, as the psalmist in Psalm 93:2 declares, "Your throne has been established from the beginning; you are from eternity."

The book of Psalms continuously points to God as King. Psalms 93, 97, and 99, for example, all start with the words, "The Lord reigns!" This declaration reminds us that God is sovereign over all. He rules with holiness and perfect righteousness. Psalm 95:6 exhorts us to respond to God's kingship by saying, "Come, let's worship and bow down; let's kneel before the Lord our Maker." God is worthy to be worshiped as King. However, we do not always worship God as we should.

Sin causes us to desire to be king—to be the ones with ultimate power and control. Throughout the Old Testament, we read about how the Israelites did not want to submit to God as their king. Instead, they desired to have human kings rule over them, just like the nations around them. Yet their decision turned out to be disastrous as most of the kings who ruled over Israel led them astray. Even King David, who encouraged Israel to worship the Lord, fell short. The failure of the kings throughout the Bible reveals that nothing good results when we desire to be the ones in complete control. However, the failure of Israel's earthly kings points us to One true King who never fails—Jesus.

Jesus is not a King who leads those in His kingdom astray. He is not a King who makes unjust decisions or prideful decrees. Jesus is the One true King because He rules with perfect righteousness. Yet Jesus is also a different kind of King, expressing His authority in ways we do not expect. Jesus left His glorious throne in heaven to put on flesh. Although He deserves glory and honor, He allowed Himself to be rejected and ridiculed. He remained silent as those around Him placed a crown of thorns on His head and a robe of purple thread around His shoulders (Mark 15:16–20). He accepted the Father's plan as He hung on the cross with a sign above His head that read "King of the Jews" (Mark 15:26).

The King of kings died for His subjects.

Though they did not bend a knee to Him, Jesus took on the punishment for the sins of mankind and died on the cross. However, three days later, Jesus rose from the dead, proclaiming His rule and reign over death. Now, because of His death and resurrection, all who trust in Jesus are brought into the kingdom of God. Though we do not deserve such a place in the King's domain, we have been granted entrance by the grace and forgiveness of Jesus.

As recipients of this grace and forgiveness, those of us who are in Christ are to dedicate our lives in worship to our great King.

Each day, we are to lay down our prideful desires to be in control and bow in submission to God. As we worship the Lord with all of who we are, we look to the day when we will see Him face to face and bow before His glorious throne. Until then, we proclaim with joy, "Now to the King eternal, immortal, invisible, the only God, be honor and glory forever and ever. Amen" (1 Timothy 1:17).

Scripture for further study

PSALM 47, MARK 15:16–32

LAMB OF GOD

There is something magical about gazing over land that has been enveloped in fresh snow. Blankets of white cover the hills and streets, untouched by the feet of little children or the blade of a snowplow. But, as the days go on, the purity of that white snow becomes tainted. Rain and dirt begin to turn the snow brown. The tires from cars blacken the snow underneath their tread. The once grandeur of perfect white is now patched with filth.

Our hearts are like tainted snow. Before sin entered the world, humanity was perfect. There was no spot of sin upon them. But when Adam and Eve sinned, the blackness of sin covered the white of righteousness. Ever since then, humanity has done all it can to make itself clean again. Yet there was nothing humans could do in their own power to cleanse themselves. However, in His kindness and grace, God created a sacrificial system designed to renew His people's hearts. On the Day of Atonement, an unblemished lamb was killed on behalf of the sins of the people. However, the sacrifice of this lamb only temporarily covered the sin.

But God had a plan. Thousands of years after God instituted the sacrificial system, a man named John saw someone coming toward him and cried out, "Here is the Lamb of God, who takes away the sin of the world!" (John 1:29 HCSB). This man is Jesus. God knew there was no earthly substitute that could permanently remove the sins of mankind—that is why He sent Jesus. Jesus is our perfect substitute. Though He took on flesh and faced the temptations of man, Jesus never sinned. He went to the cross as our unblemished and righteous Lamb. He willingly allowed Himself to be slaughtered for our sake, taking the punishment of our sins upon Him. Just as the blood of sacrificial

lambs cleansed the Israelites of their sin, so does the blood of the Lamb of God cleanse our hearts—except this time, the cleansing of Christ is everlasting.

Jesus is the only One who can make our hearts permanently clean. For those of us in Christ, we do not need to work tirelessly to maintain the purity of our hearts. The blood of Christ has made us forever new. Even when we stumble in our obedience to God and fall into sin, the forgiveness of Christ keeps our hearts clean.

When we consider the sacrifice of Jesus, the Lamb of God, our hearts should be moved to worship. Revelation 5:13 paints us a picture of our future reality when we will shout with praise, "Blessing and honor and glory and power be to the one seated on the throne, and to the Lamb, forever and ever!" Yet we can also declare these words right here and now. We did not deserve to have the blood of Jesus poured out for our sake. We did not deserve the cleansing Christ gave us through His sacrifice. May the abundant grace of the Lamb of God lead us to worship Him. May our voices be lifted in praise over these promised words fulfilled through Christ, "Though your sins are scarlet, they will be as white as snow" (Isaiah 1:18).

Scripture for further study

ISAIAH 53 AND I PETER 1:18–19

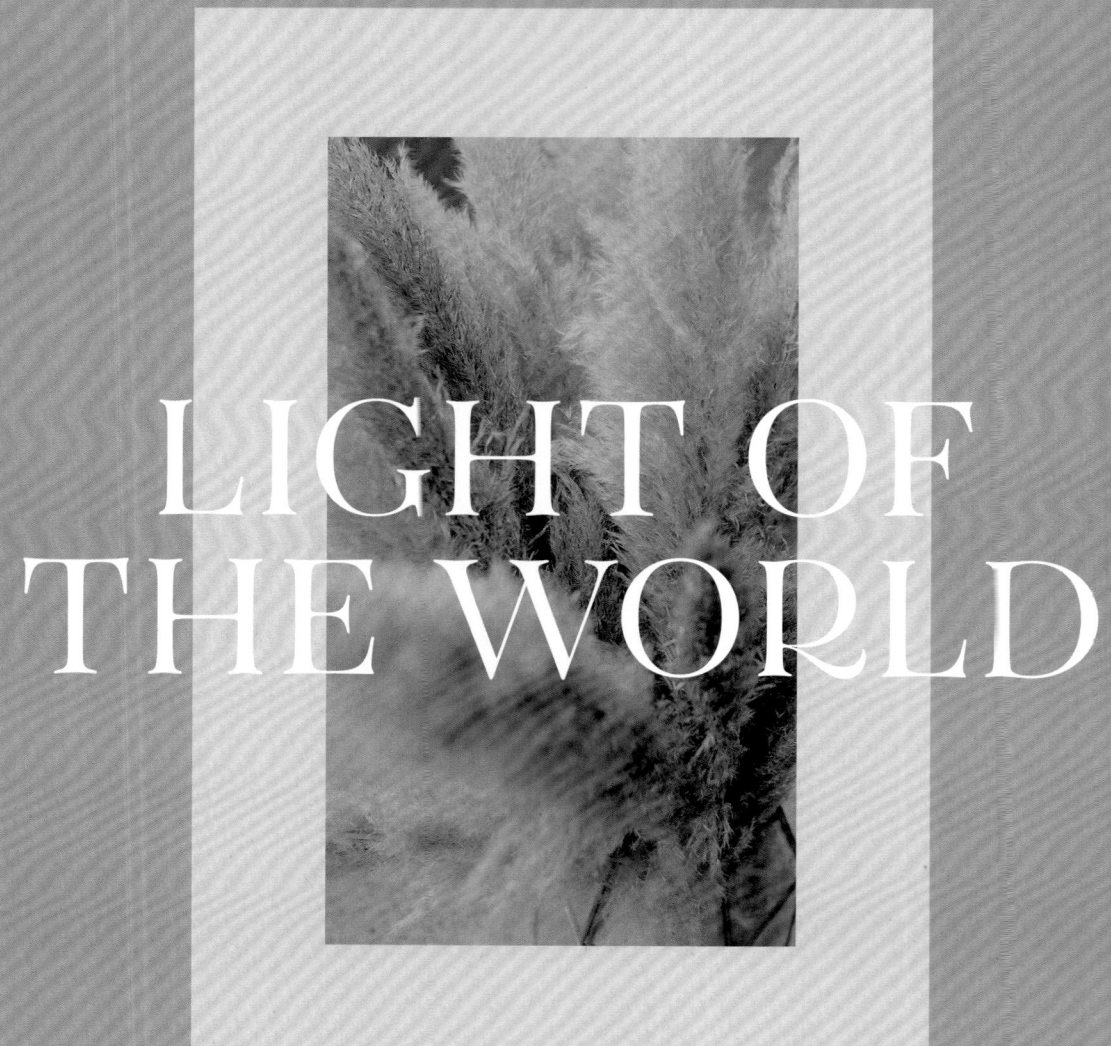

LIGHT OF THE WORLD

In the beginning, "God said, 'Let there be light,' and there was light. God saw that the light was good, and God separated the light from the darkness. God called the light 'day,' and the darkness he called 'night'" (Genesis 1:3–5). These verses from the first chapter of the Bible clearly demonstrate that God is the author of all light. He created it, He sustains it, and in His great plan, He sent an even better Light.

When Adam and Eve chose disobedience and sin entered the world in Genesis 3, a new kind of darkness inhabited the earth. But in Genesis 3:15, God promised Eve her seed would one day crush the head of Satan, and thus, a new light was promised. This new light would one day destroy the darkness of sin. Even though the sun continued to rise and set each day, the darkness of sin filled the earth.

The Bible tells us "the true light that gives light to everyone was coming into the world" (John 1:9). Jesus is this true Light, and in His perfect timing, God sent Jesus into the world. John 1:4–5 explains it this way: "In Him was life, and that life was the light of men. That light shines in the darkness, and yet the darkness did not overcome it."

Through the birth of Jesus, God once again said, "Let there be light."

The Light came to rid the world of the darkest sin and evil. The Light came to restore, reconcile, and display the glory of God.

Jesus refers to Himself as the Light of the World in the book of John. In John 8, Jesus is speaking to the Pharisees and says, "I am the light of the world. Anyone who follows me will never walk in the darkness but will have the light of life" (John 8:12).

Jesus brought the light of salvation into the world.

His perfect, sinless sacrifice on the cross destroyed the darkness caused by sin. Those who follow Christ can now enjoy the warm, pure, radiant Light that provides eternal security and abundant life. We can walk in the Light as 1 John 1:7 suggests, "If we walk in the light as he himself is in the light, we have fellowship with one another, and the blood of Jesus his Son cleanses us from all sin."

The Light cleanses us and makes us whole. It illuminates our path as we look forward to our Savior's return.

While we wait for His glorious return, Jesus calls us to be His light in the world. Believers are indwelt with the Holy Spirit, who enables us to shine the light of Christ with our lives. Jesus said in the Sermon on the Mount, "In the same way, let your light shine before others, so that they may see your good works and give glory to your Father in heaven" (Matthew 5:16). Our good works do not earn our salvation. Rather, our good works are the outpouring of love we have for our Savior who set us free from sin. We share the Light because we know what it means to be dead in our sin and made alive in Christ (Romans 6:11).

We joyfully await the day our Light returns, and darkness will be no more. When Christ comes the second time, it will be to gather His children and banish darkness forever. The book of Revelation gives us a glimpse of what life will be like in God's eternal kingdom, where "the city does not need the sun or the moon to shine on it, because the glory of God illuminates it, and its lamp is the Lamb" (Revelation 21:23). The next chapter of Revelation builds on this theme, as Scripture says, "Night will be no more; people will not need the light of a lamp or the light of the sun, because the Lord God will give them light, and they will reign forever and ever" (Revelation 22:5). What a magnificent day it will be when all things are made new, and the Light of the World will envelop us with His presence for eternity.

Scripture for further study

MATTHEW 5:14–16, JOHN 8:12–20, REVELATION 21:22–22:5

LIVING WATER

There are very few experiences that every single person shares. Time, place, and life circumstances create unique human existences for all. Yet all people—from Adam and Eve to every person walking the earth today—share a common need for water. We need water to survive because the human body is made of approximately sixty percent water. Our hearts, lungs, and brains cannot function without a steady input of water. And when we are deprived of water, our body signals that something must be done by causing us to thirst for a long, deep drink.

In the same way our physical bodies long to be hydrated with water, our souls also long to be nourished. But what satisfies a thirsty soul? We could search to the ends of the earth trying to find an answer to this question, and many have done that. Or we can simply look to the words of Jesus. As we turn to John 4, we can hear Him inviting us, just as He invited the woman at the well, to ask Him for the Living Water that will satisfy our thirst forever. Just as He told that woman, Jesus tells us, "Everyone who drinks from this water will get thirsty again. But whoever drinks from the water that I will give him will never get thirsty again. In fact, the water I will give him will become a well of water springing up in him for eternal life" (John 4:13–14).

The idea of permanently quenching the longing of our souls with the water Jesus offers is enticing but also confusing. Even the woman Jesus spoke these words to wondered where Jesus could possibly get this water from, for He had no bucket to reach down into the well He sat beside. But Jesus was not talking about a physical drink drawn from a well; instead, He was referring to His Spirit that is deposited into the hearts and souls of all who believe in Him.

Jesus used a word picture to explain what it means to trust Him as the source of life. When we are physically thirsty, we instinctively fill a cup with cold water and take a sip. But, when our souls thirst, where do we go to quench that spiritual thirst? We should go to Jesus and hold out our empty hearts, trusting that He will fill them with His Spirit, and His Spirit will satisfy us completely.

Isaiah 12:2–3 explains what it looks like for His Spirit to refresh us as it reads, "Indeed, God is my salvation; I will trust him and not be afraid, for the Lord, the Lord himself, is my strength and my song. He has become my salvation. You will joyfully draw water from the springs of salvation." The Holy Spirit continually refreshes, renews, and nourishes those who believe. His work within believers is like a spring of salvation that swells and swirls from the throne of God down to the very hearts of His people.

In Eden, God created a river, which flowed through the garden to sustain the people, plants, and animals. In His people, God gives the Holy Spirit to sustain their spiritual life. And one day, when the heavens and earth are made new, there will again be a river of life flowing from His throne. Revelation 22:1–3 describes it like this, "Then he showed me the river of the water of life, clear as crystal, flowing from the throne of God and of the Lamb down the middle of the city's main street. The tree of life was on each side of the river, bearing twelve kinds of fruit, producing its fruit every month. The leaves of the tree are for healing the nations, and there will no longer be any curse. The throne of God and of the Lamb will be in the city, and his servants will worship him." In the new heaven and new earth, we will still be sustained by the presence of God's Spirit, but from God's throne, a river will heal and sustain the tree of life and the nations.

The Living Water of God sustains all life.

Without His streams of water flowing through our dry and dusty hearts, we would never be satisfied. All those who repent and believe in Jesus are given the Holy Spirit, who perfectly and continually quenches our spiritual thirst. Praise God that He has provided us Living Water from which we can drink and be renewed each and every day.

Scripture for further study

GENESIS 1:1–12, NUMBERS 20:1–11, PSALM 63:1, ISAIAH 12:3, JEREMIAH 2:13, JOHN 4:1–15, JOHN 7:37–39, REVELATION 7:15–17, REVELATION 22:1–17

LORD OF ARMIES

The name Lord of Armies is used over 230 times in the Old Testament. However, this name of God does not appear at all in the first eight books of the Bible. Abraham, Isaac, Jacob, and Moses are never recorded calling God the Lord of Armies. But in 1 Samuel 1, we see this name ascribed to God for the first time in the story of Hannah's prayers for a miracle child to be conceived in her barren body. It is said that Hannah and her husband, Elkanah, traveled to Shiloh each year to offer a sacrifice to the Lord of Armies (1 Samuel 1:3). During this time in redemptive history, Shiloh was the place where the ark of the covenant was kept, and the priests of Israel entered the presence of the Lord. The ark was said to be the Lord's resting place. But the ark was not just an object that represented the presence of the Lord; it was also a military object. It was marched in front of the army of Israel as they went into battle, signifying the presence of the Lord with them as they crusaded forward. Israel fought on behalf of the Lord, and God's presence literally led them into battle.

The Lord also empowered Israel to prevail over its enemies. They did not fight in their own power but with His divine might and strength. Psalm 24:8 says, "Who is this King of glory? The Lord, strong and mighty, the Lord, mighty in battle."

God, being supremely sovereign, has complete control over all things. He reigns over every physical king and kingdom.

This psalm is not a euphemism; the Lord was quite literally strong and mighty in battle on behalf of His people. One well-known example of this is David's defeat of Goliath in 1 Samuel 17. David was a young man and hardly had the might or experience to defeat a hardened warrior like Goliath. Yet David reminded Goliath that though Goliath fought with sword, spear, and javelin, David fought with something more powerful—David fought with the help of the Lord of Armies (1 Samuel 17:45). And with the Lord's help, David prevailed over Goliath.

Repeatedly in Scripture, we see that the Lord is the One who handed victory to the Israelites. God is so strong in battle that when God gave the Israelites laws concerning warfare in Deuteronomy 20, the very first law was, "When you go out to war against your enemies and see horses, chariots, and an army larger than yours, do not be afraid of them, for the Lord your God, who brought you out of the land of Egypt, is with you" (Deuteronomy 20:1). God's people were not to fear, even when they were outnumbered and outmatched. They were to remember the strength of the Lord who went with them to war and be courageous because of His strength and not their own.

The Lord of Armies also rules over spiritual beings and spiritual battles. The Lord of Armies is the One who has complete control over all armies in heaven and on earth. In the New Testament, the name Lord of Armies is used only a handful of times, and it is mostly used when quoted from the Old Testament until the book of Revelation. In Revelation 19:11–20, the name Lord of Armies is not used, but rather, a description of the Lord of Armies is presented. John, the author of Revelation, describes a white horse with a rider who is called "Faithful and

True" and descends from heaven to justly judge and make war (Revelation 19:11). The armies of heaven follow Him, and with the sword from His mouth, He rules and strikes the nations. This man is Jesus, returning to earth from heaven to wage war on sin and evil.

Jesus is the Lord of Armies.

And, when He one day returns to earth, He will throw Satan, all his deceivers, and those who worship Satan into a lake of fire, where they will forever stay. Jesus will be victorious in battle on behalf of His people. He is the Lord of Armies, and all power and dominion on earth and in heaven are His!

Scripture for further study

DEUTERONOMY 20:1-4, 1 SAMUEL 1:3, 1 SAMUEL 4:4, 1 SAMUEL 17:45, PSALM 24:8-10, PSALM 80:19, ISAIAH 31:4-5, ZECHARIAH 14:1-17, REVELATION 19:11-20

MAN OF SORROWS

Imagine having the nickname Man of Sorrows. In our world, such a title might imply you are melancholy, miserable, sad, or just unhappy. Whatever description best fits the situation, it is not a name that typically emotes joy. In God's kingdom, though, the Man of Sorrows takes all despair and brings great joy.

Jesus is called the Man of Sorrows in one place in Scripture, the book of Isaiah. Isaiah 53:3 says, "He was despised and rejected by men, a man of sorrows and acquainted with grief; and as one from whom men hide their faces he was despised, and we esteemed him not" (ESV). Isaiah 53 is known as the "suffering servant" passage. In this chapter, Isaiah shares the details of Christ's life, death, and resurrection—centuries before He came to earth. As such, verse 3 points us to both a name and a description of our Savior.

Jesus is called the Man of Sorrows for several reasons. First, imagine the grief He felt when He left His glorious throne in heaven, seated next to the Father, and came to earth to live as a human. He put on earthly flesh and dwelt among sinful men, knowing what laid before Him on the cross. Second, His earthly body suffered as any human would. He felt pain, sadness, and fatigue. While He was still fully God, He was also fully man. He was tempted just as we are yet without any sin (Hebrews 4:15). Lastly, sorrow awaited Jesus as He suffered betrayal, rejection, agony, and anguish as He bore our sins on the cross. Jesus experienced the wrath we deserved and endured the punishment that was rightly ours.

Despite all the sorrow He felt, Jesus was not a sad person, for the end result of all His pain brought great joy. That end result makes us whole again by washing us white as snow. Jesus joyfully brings

us back into the presence of the Father. Hebrews 12:2 reminds us of this truth as the author writes, "For the joy that lay before him, he endured the cross, despising the shame, and sat down at the right hand of the throne of God." It brings Jesus great joy when the sorrow He endured brings His children salvation and abundant life (John 10:10).

Even though the name Man of Sorrows does not seem like a joyful name, Jesus took it and made it a name we celebrate. Calling Jesus the Man of Sorrows acknowledges His work on the cross for us. It recognizes His power to turn anguish into hope and agony into rejoicing. Whatever sorrow you face here on earth, Jesus understands and sympathizes with you. His shoulders are big enough to bear your sin and your sorrows. One day, when He returns for His children, the Man of Sorrows will have His joy made complete. In the new heavens and new earth, "He will wipe away every tear from their eyes. Death will be no more; grief, crying, and pain will be no more, because the previous things have passed away" (Revelation 21:4). Jesus will make all things new. As we wait for His return, may we rejoice in our Savior who willingly took on sorrow to bring joy to the world.

Scripture for further study

ISAIAH 53, HEBREWS 12:1-4

MIGHTY ONE

There is little that we are more aware of than our weaknesses. They permeate every area of our lives. When we fall short, it creates a ripple effect of pain through our relationships, work, and family. And most of all, our failures impact our relationships with God. We are sinners who cannot help but sin. "Weak" is a label we cannot avoid wearing. However, there is very good news for all those who are weak. The good news is that the Lord is not weak. He is strong, powerful, and mighty. And He acts with strength and might on behalf of His people because He knows they are weak. We cannot help but fall short. The Lord, however, is the Mighty One.

Often, the name Mighty One in Scripture appears as "the Mighty One of Jacob." Perhaps this is because Jacob is the first person known to use the name Mighty One, as recorded in Genesis 49:24. In this chapter, Jacob is speaking a blessing over each of his twelve sons because he knows that he will soon die. His son Joseph's blessing includes the name Mighty One to refer to God, who gave Joseph strength. Joseph's life was one marked by extreme hardship and hurt. He was sold by his brothers to slave traders and taken to Egypt, a land far away, where he worked as a slave with no hope for freedom. Even worse, he was falsely accused of a crime and unfairly imprisoned. He was a man with no freedom, no hope, and no future.

Yet God worked in Joseph's circumstances in unbelievable ways. Joseph was given the opportunity to interpret a dream Pharaoh had that was greatly troubling him. God gave Joseph wisdom to understand this dream, and as a result, Joseph was promoted to be second in command of all of Egypt. Years later, God also providentially reunited and reconciled Joseph to his brothers and father. Jacob declared that Joseph was able to overcome all that he encountered in his life because the Mighty One strengthened him to do so. God, strong in power and might, used all Joseph experienced for good.

There is no one more capable than the Lord.

We see the name Mighty One mentioned again in the book of Isaiah. Isaiah wrote to the people of Judah before and during their capture and exile. The people had been desperately sinful, and God allowed them to be taken captive and led away from their homes as a result. In Isaiah 1:24, "the Mighty One of Israel" promised to use His power against His people to punish them for their sins, as they rightly deserved.

Later, in Isaiah 49:26, the Lord is talking about the future restoration of Israel. God allowed His people to experience the consequences of their sin, yet He also planned to redeem them from their brokenness and shame. God promised to repay the nations who plundered them and took them captive. He promised to buy Judah's freedom again so that all people—those in Judah and those watching from the outside—would know that God is indeed the Mighty One of Jacob and Judah. Finally, in Isaiah 60:16, God told Judah that once He freed and restored them, the nations who once harmed Judah would be the very nations that would care for them. The Lord can do anything. He is stronger and more powerful than the mightiest kingdoms and kings. He and He alone is the Mighty One.

The Mighty One of Jacob uses His infinite power to providentially care for His people. He is their protection and strength in all things. He always uses His power justly, and that includes handing down consequences when required. He also uses His power according to His wisdom and knowledge, which means He does not always use it to prevent harm. Instead, He sometimes uses His might to strengthen those experiencing challenges and difficulty. He also rescues His people from harm in the right time and way, and He redeems the harm they experience for good.

Jesus is the ultimate way God has shown His might and power to His people.

God sent Jesus at the right time, when we were still weak and still sinners, so His power would be made known to us. As much as we are aware of our weaknesses, may we also be aware of the surpassing strength and power of the Mighty One—the Savior He sent to save us from our sin and give us eternal life with Him.

Scripture for further study

GENESIS 49:24, PSALM 132:1–5, ISAIAH 1:24, ISAIAH 49:26, ISAIAH 60:16

MOST HIGH

Who are the authority figures in your life? They are most likely people such as your boss at work, a mentor, a pastor, a parent, or a coach. These people define the spaces in which we encounter them. A team will rise or fall based on the investment of its coach. Households are built up or torn down by the parents who oversee them. Leaders matter. Their temperaments, words, and actions define the environments in which they lead. But every human leader, no matter how high and powerful they seem, is ultimately subordinate to the Lord Most High. God is above all. He alone is elevated, exalted, and incomparable in His power and glory. Just as an earthly leader's nature defines the small sphere in which he or she leads,

God is the One leader from whom the whole earth finds its definition.

God is who He says He is. The earth is what God says it is. And we are who God says we are because He is ultimately and completely above all. God Most High is the One who is surpassingly wise, true, righteous, and just. What He says is what is. He simply spoke creation into being. He said, "let there be," and there was. He alone has command of all the world from His heavenly throne.

Abraham was a man who understood the power of the Most High God. In Genesis 14:18–22, we see the name Most High given to the Lord for the first time by Melchizedek and Abram, whose name God would later change to Abraham. At this point in redemptive history, Abram had just defeated four large and powerful kingdoms with a small army of only 318 men. He had rescued his cousin, Lot, who had been plundered and captured by these large armies. Immediately after his victory, two kings came to visit Abram. One is Melchizedek, who was likely the king of Jerusalem and was referred to as a priest and a righteous man (Hebrews 7:2). Melchizedek recognized the incredible way the God Most High had led Abram to victory, and he blessed Abram.

In contrast, another king, the unrighteous king from Sodom, approached Abram. Abram had recovered land, goods, and people who belonged to Sodom when he defeated the four powerful kings. The king of Sodom told Abram he could keep all the goods he had recaptured in battle if he would only give back the people. He was probably offering Abram a considerable fortune. But Abram, likely realizing the unrighteousness of the king of Sodom, refused his offer. He did not want any of these goods that came by way of unrighteousness. He said, "I have raised my hand in an oath to the Lord, God Most High, Creator of heaven and earth, that I will not take a thread or sandal strap or anything that belongs to you, so you can never say, 'I made Abram rich'" (Genesis 14:22b–23).

Abram knew the king of Sodom was powerful, and the wealth the king was offering him was considerable, but Abram recognized the Lord was more powerful. The God Most High had given him instructions on war and spoils of war, and Abram honored those instructions, knowing that God would take care of him better than any amount of money could. Believing that God is the Lord Most High includes trusting and obeying His ways. God's ways are not the ways of man. God's thoughts are not the thoughts of man. God is high above, and He thinks and acts according to His exalted and elevated knowledge.

Incredibly, in His infinite knowledge, God sent Jesus, who was called the Son of the Most High, to the earth to live and die so that we might receive forgiveness for our sins. In Luke 1:32–35, an angel explains to Mary that by the Holy Spirit, the power of the Most High will overshadow her and conceive in her a baby who would be the Savior of the world. God used His vast power to come near to us. The Most High God sent His Son to us. Jesus taught, preached, healed, and helped people during His earthly life in power. He submitted to death in power. And miraculously, He was raised to new life in power so that those who believe in Him might also enter into new life through the power of His blood cleansing our sins. The Most High God is also the God who came close. He created all, knows all, and is all-powerful, yet Jesus yielded His power so that through Him we might draw near to the Father. The Lord Most High is so worthy of our worship, obedience, and love—now and forevermore.

Scripture for further study

GENESIS 14:18–22, PSALM 21:7, PSALM 57:2, PSALM 78:56, PSALM 83:18, ISAIAH 14:14, DANIEL 4:25, LUKE 1:32–35, LUKE 1:76, LUKE 6:35

PRINCE OF PEACE

There are moments when worry floods our minds, fear grips our hearts, and panic surges through our bodies. We struggle to calm our racing thoughts, release the tension we feel, and take a breath. Each one of us experiences anxiety in one shape or form because we live in a deeply broken world. The sinfulness of this world brings trauma, troubles, and trials that cause us to be afraid. And because of the fear and anxiety we feel, we often long for any semblance of peace.

Yet God has not left fearful humanity without a source of peace. Thousands of years ago, God spoke these words through the prophet Isaiah: "For a child will be born for us, a son will be given to us, and the government will be on his shoulders. He will be named Wonderful Counselor, Mighty God, Eternal Father, Prince of Peace" (Isaiah 9:6). Although God's people were broken and burdened, they could have hope, knowing that one day a child would be born who would bring them peace. While it took many years of waiting, God was faithful to fulfill His promise. On an ordinary night in a small stable, the Prince of Peace was born—Jesus.

The peace that Jesus provides is a peace that all of us crave but do not know we need. The word for "peace" in Isaiah 9:6 is the Hebrew word *šālôm*. This *šālôm* peace, also discussed on page 141, describes a sense of completeness—of brokenness being repaired once again. While we often crave peace for relief, the peace that Jesus provides ultimately provides restoration. Each one of us is separated from God because of our sin. Instead of perfect peace, there is wrath between us and God. There is nothing we can do on our own to remedy this broken relationship and satisfy God's wrath. Yet our Prince of Peace went to the cross and took the

No longer do we have to search for a source of peace, for we have found peace in Christ.

punishment we deserve for our sin. The blood of Jesus covers the guilt of our sin and satisfies God's wrath. Because of the sacrifice of Jesus, those who trust and believe in Him have peace with God.

The restoration we have received from Jesus brings us relief. No longer do we have to search for a source of peace, for we have found peace in Christ. This peace Jesus provides impacts our everyday lives. Although we live in a world that causes us fear, we can rest in the peace of God. The peace we possess in Christ allows us to view what we are experiencing with an eternal perspective. Even if our worst fears are realized, we know that because our future with Christ remains secure, we are going to be okay. Ultimately, we know that we will be okay because God's Word promises that Jesus will make all things new. One day, our Prince of Peace will return to remove all sin and suffering from the earth. There will be no more fear, worry, or anxiety—only everlasting peace.

The peace we possess in Christ also comforts us in moments of anxiety. The peace of God that comes over us in times of fear slows our racing thoughts, relieves our tension, and enables us to take a breath. Although anxiety can be a weighty battle, God's peace flows stronger than the flood of fear. If you find yourself anxious today, come to the God who gives you His peace. Ask to experience the comfort and rest that is found in Him. In every moment of worry and fear, the Prince of Peace is near.

Scripture for further study

JOHN 14:27, ROMANS 5:1, EPHESIANS 2:14

RABBI

Students calling their teachers by their first names is often seen as a sign of disrespect. In many parts of the world, students are to call their teachers Mr., Mrs., or Ms. out of respect for their authority and position. In Jewish culture, students and community members refer to the spiritual leaders in their synagogues as Rabbi, or Teacher. Rabbi is a title that communicates "my master." This is a title of authority and utmost respect. While Jesus went about His earthly ministry, He was referred to as Rabbi. Jesus did not ask to be called this name, but His actions throughout His ministry led people to call Him Rabbi. From the very beginning of His ministry, Jesus designated Himself as a spiritual teacher. He taught in the synagogue and traveled around teaching crowds of people about the Word of God.

However, Jesus was a different kind of Rabbi from those in the Jewish community. Jesus did not gain His authority from His education; Jesus had the authority to teach the Word of God because He is God. The truths that Jesus spoke on earth were from the very lips of God. While some saw Jesus as only a spiritual teacher, others noticed there was something about Jesus that was unique. John 1:49 records this response to Jesus: "'Rabbi,' Nathanael replied, 'You are the Son of God; you are the King of Israel!'" Similarly, when Jesus was approached by a Pharisee named Nicodemus, Nicodemus said to Him, "Rabbi, we know that you are a teacher who has come from God, for no one could perform these signs you do unless God were with him" (John 3:2).

Many people in our world today view Jesus solely as a good moral teacher. In their eyes, He is on the same level as Rabbis today — someone we can admire and who has spiritual truths from which we can learn. Just like those in Jesus's time, peo-

Jesus's teachings were not meant to remain in one's mind but cut to one's heart.

ple today may respect Jesus as a teacher but deny any claim of His divinity. Sadly, what these people miss is that Jesus did not come to simply teach spiritual truths but to bring salvation. Jesus's teachings were not meant to remain in one's mind but cut to one's heart. Through His words, and ultimately through His death and resurrection, Jesus declares that salvation from sin is possible through Him. Those who believe that Jesus is the Son of God have the opportunity to receive the salvation He offers.

For those of us who are followers of Christ, we can sit at the feet of our great Rabbi each day. Just as students respect and listen to their teachers, so are we to open God's Word with a posture of humble submission. As believers, we are to be pupils who are not only hearers of the Word of God but doers of the Word of God (James 1:22). Like a student who cannot wait to put into practice what she learned in her lesson, so are we to live out what God's Word commands joyfully. And, like a teacher who sits with us and helps us learn, we have the Holy Spirit inside us, who illuminates God's Word. The Holy Spirit connects the truths of God's Word to our hearts, guiding us and empowering us to obey the Lord. As we go out into the world, we use the Word of God to show others how Jesus is more than just a good moral teacher. When people sit at the feet of Jesus, they have the opportunity to have their hearts cleansed and their lives transformed forever.

Scripture for further study

MATTHEW 7:24–29, MARK 1:21–22, LUKE 10:38–42

SAVIOR

What makes a compelling story? Think about your favorite novel or movie and why you love it. You might think about the characters, the location, or the time period, but the story itself hinges on a specific key element—conflict. What is the problem that needs to be resolved by the end of the story? When we read a good story, we are drawn into the characters' lives, hoping for a satisfying conclusion to their story and the book itself.

The story of Scripture is no different. In the garden of Eden, conflict was born as sin entered God's world. Nothing was left untouched by its effects. Relationships were fractured. Rebellion took root. All throughout the pages of Scripture, people waited and longed for resolution to the conflict that arose from Eden, wondering how the story would conclude. Would they be rescued? Would the brokenness ever be restored? Would their story have a happy ending? As we read, our hearts cry out with theirs, longing for a Savior.

A new chapter in their story reveals a glimmer of hope. In Luke 1, a young woman named Mary gets word that a Savior is indeed coming: "You will conceive and give birth to a son, and you will name him Jesus. He will be great and will be called the Son of the Most High, and the Lord God will give him the throne of his father David. He will reign over the house of Jacob forever, and his kingdom will have no end" (Luke 1:31–33). Imagine how overwhelming that must have been for Mary—to hear that the long-awaited Messiah would arrive in her lifetime but would also be born into her family. After Jesus's birth, a group of nearby shepherds received the same message when an angel stood before them and said, "Today in the city of David a Savior was born for you, who is the Messiah, the Lord" (Luke 2:11). The angels were

*Our hope is not in ourselves;
it is in Jesus Christ, the
Savior of the world.*

clear about the identity of this child—He is the Son of the Most High, Savior, Messiah, and Lord. There is no mistaking what has taken place. The Savior is here.

We know where the story goes from there. Jesus grew up and lived a perfect and holy life. But then He went to the cross and suffered a horrible death. At the time, God's people felt like this was not how their story was supposed to go. How is the death of their Messiah a happy ending to their story? The only way to salvation was through a perfect substitute. No amount of good works can earn us eternal life. Even while we were dead in our sins, Christ made us alive by His glorious grace (Ephesians 2:4–5). Through the Savior, we are given the gift of salvation (Titus 2:11). We now have a new identity (2 Corinthians 5:17), a new family (1 Peter 2:9–10), and a new eternity (John 3:16).

The story of God's people is one of peace, conflict, and restoration. It centers around the hero, Jesus our Savior, who entered into human existence and conquered death once and for all. He invites us into this incredible story of redemption. We can quit our strivings and release the burden of trying to be our own savior. Our hope is not in ourselves; it is in Jesus Christ, the Savior of the world.

Scripture for further study

HOSEA 13:4, LUKE 2, ACTS 13:23, 1 TIMOTHY 4:10, TITUS 2:11–14

SHIELD

When going into battle, a soldier must be prepared. As a vital part of an ancient soldier's armor, a good shield provided protection when under attack. Historians suggest that many of the shields soldiers used in ancient Rome were curved rather than a typical flat design. The rounded front of the shield would ensure that anything that hit them would be deflected away with less impact on the soldier. But the soldier's safety was only as sure as the shield itself. Without that protection, he was without hope.

All throughout the Bible, we see glimpses of God acting as a Shield for His people. In Genesis 15, God comes to Abraham, then called Abram, in a vision. He is commanded not to fear because God says He will be a Shield for Abram. In turn, God promises a great reward through offspring as numerous as the stars in the sky. God will be faithful to fulfill His promise through Abram. Abram was secure in God, his Shield, trusting God to keep His word.

Just before his death, Moses shared one last message of blessing and hope for the tribes of Israel in Deuteronomy 33. "How happy you are, Israel! Who is like you, a people saved by the Lord? He is the shield that protects you, the sword you boast in. Your enemies will cringe before you, and you will tread on their backs" (Deuteronomy 33:29). Moses reminded them earlier in the book that they were chosen by God as a people for His own possession (Deuteronomy 7:6). Their protection is rooted in their identity as a people saved by God. Not only is God their Shield, but He is also their Sword. It is in the very nature of God to protect, defend, and fight for His people.

In Psalm 18, David vividly describes the providential care of the Lord. David's life was in danger at many points, and this psalm

In Christ alone, we find strength and security. Nothing else in this world will provide refuge for our weary souls.

mirrors 2 Samuel 22 when David recounts the ways that God has shielded him from his enemies. God is called a Shield multiple times in these two chapters of Scripture. David praises God as "my shield, the horn of my salvation, my stronghold, my refuge, and my Savior…" (2 Samuel 22:3). God was David's Shield in a very tangible sense. God was faithful to preserve David's life as he was delivered from the hands of his enemies.

We may not be physically hiding from our enemies like David, but we seek protection from circumstances constantly. We want to maintain good health. We want our families to be safe. We want our finances to be secure. These are not bad things to desire, but we are not ultimately in control. We cannot fully prepare ourselves for every situation we will face in this life. But we can take comfort in our sovereign, loving, all-knowing, unchanging God. The King of kings laid down His life by going to the cross, bearing our sins on His shoulders, and shielding us from the penalty we deserve. In Christ alone, we find strength and security. Nothing else in this world will provide refuge for our weary souls. When under attack, take cover in Jesus. He is our strong and trustworthy Shield, and those who look to Him will never be ashamed (Psalm 34:5).

Scripture for further study

DEUTERONOMY 33, PSALM 18, PSALM 28:7, PSALM 91:4, PSALM 119:114

STRONG TOWER

When you hear the word "tower," you might picture a medieval castle or a palace from your favorite childhood movie. Whatever the mental picture, a tower evokes feelings of strength, safety, bravery, and courage. In the Old Testament, towers were typically a part of a wall that fortified the city. The tower was used as a lookout to spot an approaching enemy, and it gave soldiers the advantage of height from which to rain down weapons. Whenever an enemy was spotted, those outside the city walls would be called to flee into the city gates and seek protection from the tower. This picture perfectly describes how God cares for His children.

In Proverbs 18:10, the wise King Solomon wrote, "The name of the Lord is a strong tower; the righteous run to it and are protected." As the king of Israel, Solomon understood the importance of a fortified city against one's enemies. Israel had many foes, and a mighty fortress was important for protection. Speaking of God as a Strong Tower was Solomon's way of describing God's nature as high above man, stronger than any enemy, and a refuge for all who call on Him.

King David, Solomon's father, also wrote, "I call to you from the ends of the earth when my heart is without strength. Lead me to a rock that is high above me, for you have been a refuge for me, a strong tower in the face of the enemy" (Psalm 61:2–3). David was a man of war who conquered other nations and had many enemies. He, too, understood the necessity of having a God who was high above everything—a God who provided a secure fortress in His presence and refuge from enemies. Our Strong Tower is God Almighty, who faithfully cares for His children in every storm or battle of life.

Our Strong Tower is God Almighty, who faithfully cares for His children in every storm or battle of life.

It is important for us to remember that the Strong Tower protects the righteous. Only those who seek the Lord and trust in Christ are made righteous. The pure blood of Jesus makes us right before our holy God. The Lord is a stronghold and refuge because whoever calls on His name will be safe in His arms forever. The prophet Joel prophesied to the people of Judah about the terrible Day of the Lord when judgment would rain down on all who rebelled against God. Yet, in his prophecy, Joel provided hope for the people when he said, "Then everyone who calls on the name of the Lord will be saved" (Joel 2:32). Salvation is given to those who call on the mighty name of the Lord. The apostles Peter and Paul understood Joel's prophecy as pointing to Jesus. In both Acts 2:21 and Romans 10:13, this verse from Joel is used to point people to salvation through Christ alone. Once you place your heart in the safety of Christ's loving arms, you are secure in the strong tower of the Lord. One day, when Christ returns and judgment is poured out upon those who rebelled against God, you will be at peace because you ran to the Strong Tower and were saved by the righteous blood of Jesus.

Scripture for further study

PSALM 61, PROVERBS 18:10, ACTS 2:14–24, ROMANS 10:1–13

THE VINE

The Bible is filled with farming imagery. From the moment the garden was created and Adam and Eve became its caretakers, to the present day in which farming across the globe is how we fill stomachs, toiling the land is part of life. It only makes sense that the pages of Scripture are filled with metaphors and similes that remind us who God is in light of the seed, the work, and the harvest. Jesus specifically used farming language and examples throughout His earthly ministry. In John 15, Jesus is nearing His arrest and crucifixion. His message, as recorded in this chapter, prepares His disciples for what life serving Him will look like once He conquers death and ascends into heaven. To do this, Jesus points His disciples to an example they likely walked past each day: the vineyard.

In John 15:1, 5, Jesus says, "I am the true vine, and my Father is the gardener. . . . I am the vine; you are the branches. The one who remains in me and I in him produces much fruit, because you can do nothing without me." Immediately, Jesus sets up the picture of a gardener working in a vineyard. God is the Gardener who plants the vineyard. Jesus is the true Vine that will never wither or die, and those who follow Him are the branches whose life is sustained only through the Vine. Jesus's message is twofold for the disciples and for us as believers today.

First, we have to remember that life is found and sustained by the Vine. Only in Christ will we find true hope, joy, peace, and salvation. In a vineyard, when a branch is no longer attached to the vine, it withers and dies and is thrown into the fire. So it is for anyone who does not have faith in Christ. The gardener prunes those branches that no longer remain in the vine. They are not useful or viable for the harvest. Apart from Christ, we can do nothing (John 15:5). We must rely on His life-giving, life-sustaining grace to have abundant life.

Secondly, followers of Christ are called to produce fruit. A branch that is attached to the vine will produce much fruit as it was designed to do. Jesus enables us to produce fruit for His kingdom. Through your relationship with Him, your study of Scripture, prayer, and fellowship with other believers, you have everything you need to grow and produce much fruit for the glory of the Lord. The Holy Spirit also enables you to produce the fruit of "love, joy, peace, patience, kindness, goodness, faithfulness, gentleness, and self-control" (Galatians 5:22–23). The works we do for Christ are not to earn favor; they are an outpouring of our love for Him and the life we find in Him.

When you remain in the Vine, the harvest will be plentiful.

In the gospels, Jesus often shares a parable or story and then follows with an explanation to emphasize His point. He does the same here, very clearly telling the disciples what they are to do. "This is my command: Love one another as I have loved you. No one has greater love than this: to lay down his life for his friends. You are my friends if you do what I command you" (John 15:12–14). Jesus is the true Vine where we find life. Once we find that life, we are to love others just as He does, and we are to do as He commands. In one of his letters, the Apostle John reminds us of the truths Jesus taught, writing, "Whoever confesses that Jesus is the Son of God—God remains in him and he in God.

And we have come to know and to believe the love that God has for us. God is love, and the one who remains in love remains in God, and God remains in him" (1 John 4:15–16).

Remain in the Vine, for it is there you will find life!

Scripture for further study

JOHN 15:1–17, 1 JOHN 4:7–5:4

WONDERFUL COUNSELOR

A traveler comes to an intersection on a desert highway. As the tumbleweeds drift across the landscape, she ponders what direction to take. She can either continue on the road she is heading or turn on a different way. The road ahead is familiar, but coyotes, snakes, and other creatures roam the area at night. The road to her right is unknown, but she sees no signs of trouble ahead. Dusk is approaching, so she must decide. Conflicted, she needs counsel.

Humanity faces crossroads in life. We encounter decisions and circumstances which reveal that, on our own, we do not have the ability to choose wisely. In our sin, we chose the road leading to coyotes and snakes rather than the road leading to life with God. Our souls constantly need counsel.

When was the last time you sought counsel? Did you do so openly or with hesitance? Were you willing to listen to the counselor's advice, or did you question it? Some of us may have mentors, therapists, parents, or friends we seek out for advice. Others of us may not have such a community and feel like we are navigating life lost and confused. On the contrary, a few of us may be surrounded by trusted advisers but fail to heed their wisdom because of pride. Whatever group we fall into, there is a God who is called the Wonderful Counselor and intervenes in every situation to direct us with His insight. The name Wonderful Counselor conveys that God's guidance leads to both practical wisdom and incomprehensible truth.

The idea of divine counsel is present in the Old Testament. The Lord established judges and kings to direct His people in the Word. Using discretion and sound judgment, these leaders made decisions on civil disputes. In their efforts, they reflected the incomprehensible wisdom of God. For example, by God's grace,

The name Wonderful Counselor conveys that God's guidance leads to both practical wisdom and incomprehensible truth.

King Solomon was known to be the wisest king (1 Kings 4:30). Solomon passed on his wisdom through proverbs. The book of Proverbs contains short, wise sayings. As one of the wisdom literature books of Scripture, it offers practical advice for the day-to-day while pointing to the eternal truth of God's salvific plan. But Solomon and the other writers of Proverbs were still impaired by sin. Their fallenness made their wisdom imperfect, and even Solomon chose to travel down a road far away from God.

But divine counsel was fulfilled in the person of Jesus Christ. Jesus is called the Wonderful Counselor in Isaiah 9:6. As God in the flesh, Jesus possesses the fullness of wisdom. During His time on earth, Jesus never sinned and always chose to worship the Lord. With His words, ministry, and saving work, Jesus led people back to God. And after His ascension to His heavenly throne, Jesus sent us another Counselor: the Holy Spirit.

The Holy Spirit, the Spirit of Jesus Himself, takes up residence in our hearts when we place our faith in Christ. By His indwelling presence, He stirs up wisdom in us so that we surrender to the Lord. With His help, we loosen the grip we had on our plans for our careers, relationships, and daily activities. Then, we seek God's will and meditate on the wonderful truth of the gospel as we navigate life. In all situations, we can humbly ask for Jesus's divine counsel, knowing that His guidance is what we need.

Scripture for further study

PSALM 32:8, PSALM 73:24, ISAIAH 9:6, ISAIAH 29:14,
JOHN 14:16–17, JOHN 14:26, JOHN 16:7–14

YAHWEH

An elderly woman sits in her rocking chair and reaches for some home movies on cassette tapes. The woman wipes the dust off the film and loads a tape into the player. As she watches, she hears the name of a past loved one being called in the background. Amazement and joy overwhelm her heart. This name of the past leads her to reflect. Through the memories, she recalls the person's character and the experiences they shared. She ends the video but hides such a name in her heart. She does not voice the name to others, treasuring it instead as a sacred symbol of times long ago.

The description above illustrates how the Israelites responded to God's name, Yahweh. *Yahweh* is a Hebrew word that means "He is." For the ancient people, Yahweh was representative of God working in redemptive history to accomplish salvation. It caused the Israelites to remember a time when the true God of the universe met with Moses and called him to deliver them from Egyptian slavery. For instance, in Exodus 3:13, Moses asked God what name he should give the Israelite elders when they inquired about the divine being who sent him. God responded with "I AM WHO I AM" and told Moses to say, "I AM has sent me to you" (Exodus 3:14). In Hebrew, I AM is translated as *Ehyeh*.

While slaves in Egypt, the Israelites were surrounded by many gods and goddesses—creatures crafted into idol statues. The Israelites may have grown accustomed to Egyptian idols with distinct names and abilities. But through *Ehyeh*, God reminded His covenant people who the real God was. He reminded them that He was incomparable to all other spiritual beings. He revealed that He was all-encompassing and not limited to a particular attribute or power.

The Israelites addressed God's all-encompassing nature as Yahweh, or "He is." They viewed this name as the most sacred of them all. In antiquity, Yahweh was never spoken or written fully. Rather, people said *Adonai*, the Hebrew word for "Lord", and wrote the shorthand *YHWH*. But the listeners and readers knew what name was being conveyed, and they were in awe. In their hearts, they remembered the covenant God and His plan of salvation.

For believers today, the divine name Yahweh continues to relay God's eternality, mystery, absoluteness, independence, objectivity, and supremacy.

When the idols of culture distract us and our minds drift from the truth, we can remember God is better than anything the world offers. He is more than anything we can capture in words. And we can look to Jesus, through whom Yahweh made His all-encompassing nature visible.

Jesus often used the Greek phrase *ego eimi*, which means "I exist" or "I am." In this phrase, He aligned Himself with the divine name *Ehyeh*, or Yahweh. Jesus showed that the same vast God of old, the One who talked with Moses, was present in His flesh. And this time, Yahweh was here to save His people from slavery to sin.

Yahweh might not be a word we say often. In some recent translations of Scripture, Yahweh is not specified but denoted as "Lord." Still, when reading or saying "Lord," we should respond with amazement and joy at this sacred name. Then, we can recall the salvation that the true God of the universe accomplished.

Ultimately, when we hold the whisper of Yahweh in our hearts, we remember the name that is above all other names: Jesus.

Scripture for further study
EXODUS 3:13–15, DEUTERONOMY 4:35, JOHN 13:19